# MECHANOPHILIA

## BOOK 1

# M E C H A N

**Sarah Burgoyne**

# OPHILIA

## BOOK 1

Vi Khi Nao

**An imprint
of Anvil Press**

Anvil Press Publishers Inc.
P.O. Box 3008, Station Terminal
Vancouver, BC V6B 3X5
www.anvilpress.com

Cover design: Rayola.com
Interior design & typesetting: Stuart Ross
Author photos by Laurence Philomene (Sarah Burgoyne) and
    Scott Indermaur (Vi Khi Nao)
The images inside this book were created with the assistance of DALL·E 2.

feed dog logo: Catrina Longmuir

Printed and bound in Canada

Library and Archives Canada Cataloguing in Publication

Title: Mechanophilia. Book 1 / Sarah Burgoyne, Vi Khi Nao.
Names: Burgoyne, Sarah, author. | Nao, Vi Khi, 1979- author.
Description: First edition.
Identifiers: Canadiana 20230564453 | ISBN 9781772142198 (softcover)
Subjects: LCGFT: Poetry.
Classification: LCC PS8603.U73715 M43 2023 | DDC C811/.6—dc23

Represented in Canada by Publishers Group Canada
Distributed in Canada by Raincoast Books; in the U.S. by Small Press
Distribution (SPD)

The publisher gratefully acknowledges the financial assistance of the
Canada Council for the Arts, the Canada Book Fund, and the Province
of British Columbia through the B.C. Arts Council and the Book
Publishing Tax Credit.

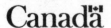  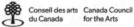

I thought that if I could put it all down, that would be one way. And next the thought came to me that to leave all out would be another, and truer, way.

—John Ashbery, *Three Poems*

*Love Song Between Darkness and Light*

3    The scene breaks
.

1    I
4    dreamed I saw us
1    through
5    the window of a blue
9    refrigerator made of fabrics from Sri Lanka and
       Alaska.
2    The plenum
6    made me stand arduously outside the
5    broken capillaries delicately arranged on
3    your sad face.
5    You're seven years younger than
8    the cypress tree with long limbs that extend
9    into a movie where they perform erratic green
       calligraphy.
7    My eyes, my heart—these silhouettes of
9    the dash, ink night's stutter into the day's rush.
3    Ash for your
2    cellophane tray.
3    Ash for your
8    gold pile of spinnable hay, your lackaday birdsong,
4    your ambush for red
6    physical width. For puzzles and lakes
2    bearing timelessness
6    the only possible customers are your
4    morose silence and resilience.
3    Your deserted perfume
3    has fallen asleep
8    with breath and dreams that reek of wine

3   soaked in amnesia.

2   The darkness

7   sits with its black toes dipped in

9   the presence of illusion—the night a fantastic robot

5   for outlining metaphors of rebirth.

0   The obtuse flutes of the born rippling reeds—each a
zero,

2   a nightingale

8   wind-toppled, fold their emblematic potential into
time's slurry.

8   Memory of being youthful near a mirthful caress

4   stained by grass song.

1   I

9   plant my green grammar in the open sky of

7   your clavicle. The ocean meets my knotted

1   sorrow

6   riding its melancholic horse briskly past

9   desire. Desire, yes, is how cumulus clouds occupy
space.

3   Won't you take

9   my mistake, which was desire, to further inflate
emptiness?

9   Won't you take my heirloom of rubescent tomatoes
with

3   suitable prayers, aflame?

7   Won't you take me through your night

5   to write in clear ink

1   a

0   tundra's eulogy?

5   Won't you take me with

8   the terriblest conclusion: that all is urgently bland.

2   This rupture

| | |
|---|---|
| 0 | of two or three square miles |
| 9 | of tears striates across a river rewritten by a |
| 7 | city shape. A foolish pitch to cancel |
| 4 | my membership with loneliness. |
| 9 | Something hit our heads and tiptoed into cirrus clouds |
| 4 | while desolate rain memorized |
| 4 | imperfect geometries, letting fall |
| 5 | devastating isotopes of emotional indifference |
| 9 | in the same place. You, in pristine ditches, find |
| 2 | an absolute |
| 3 | tangle spreading apart |
| 0 | eyelids from dreams. |
| 7 | Fresh pigments of unasked questions fan across |
| 8 | your lips. Private colours I will crush slowly, |
| 1 | thoroughly, |
| 6 | against the basin of your hipbone, |
| 4 | blushingly forgetting my name. |
| 0 | How could you |
| 6 | tell me infinity's page is asway, |
| 2 | near delirium, |
| 8 | among mountains? I have heard a remnant of |
| 6 | muted daffodils soaked in a corona |
| 2 | of elegiac |
| 0 | algebra. |
| 8 | Your sumptuous vacuity steps out of the theatre |
| 9 | while I watch you delete your small soft-spoken footsteps. |
| 9 | An imperceptible rip in the stocking of my mood |
| 8 | isn't to be expected from the precious milieu |
| 6 | sinking stars deep inside summer's laundry— |
| 2 | basket of |

8    papercuts orbiting my sleep. Lines repeat in space

0    travelling among hemoglobins.

3    A red-winged shift

4    of contracted subunits gathers

8    tapetum lucinda—the opal night gaze—of twilit

2    breasts hovering

5    like letters or periods of

3    withdrawal as I

4    double into mirrors and

2    painful inflections.

1    Moments

1    cast

7    in camo silks round into poised myths.

0    I want us to

6    speak in vowels only, to surround

7    the vascular parlour of our isolated mouths

9    with a counterworld of marbles rolled over and over.

8    Outside the air is casual and old; I

2    garland it

1    quietly

4    mooring hair and breath.

8    The strong wind unlocks zephyrs of senselessness
       within

0    my touch. Fingers circus toward

8    the dilapidated bark overlaying the lavish young patina.

6    Wrists of trees, their lapped muscles

5    fibrous and decisive against the

1    ascendent

3    imperial cheekbone of

2    shattered harmonies

8    float my eyesight down a glazed, fragmented river.

2    Itinerant grottoes,

| | |
|---|---|
| 3 | nomadic accented cathedrals |
| 0 | in close-up, spread open. |
| 6 | The ardour of smoke and fire |
| 6 | splits my equivocations in tangled disobedience |
| 4 | as if I am |
| 7 | unsure of its sun-embroidered gospel. I want |
| 0 | your bread on my tablecloth |
| 9 | the way I would see it if your enemy |
| 3 | were ready to |
| 8 | hold that nothing they know of you is |
| 4 | myth beneath smothered ash |
| 4 | but rather myth's ember |
| 6 | severed and discontinued by the equipoise |
| 0 | of your own questions sweating up and exploding into flight. |
| 9 | Must I be the cold kettle you can't pour |
| 5 | without my answer beating under |
| 5 | the floorboard? I elevate my |
| 0 | tongue without messages near |
| 5 | a wilderness camp full of |
| 8 | the sounds omitted by sleep—each younger than |
| 2 | fen water. |
| 2 | Terse mirages |
| 3 | coruscate on the |
| 1 | idyllic |
| 7 | yellow afternoon of your rustic semi-lambent thirst. |
| 2 | Must I |
| 5 | ambush your taste buds with |
| 3 | thousands of lilacs |
| 5 | or take your debilitating ocean |
| 9 | estranged even from yourself for the future song of |
| 4 | the suppressed and long-forgotten |

| | |
|---|---|
| 0 | like a garment worn inside the body |
| 8 | of my memory as if to cross-dress an |
| 1 | orchid? |
| 2 | Yes, to |
| 8 | orbit your home in blue silk then red. |
| 4 | Lipsticks chase the throat |
| 8 | of the half-life of lust—its gnawed selvage |
| 1 | impulsively |
| 1 | threshed. |
| 1 | Pulsate |
| 7 | into recessed eclipses masking netted careening animals. |
| 4 | Maniacally dance without hooves |
| 5 | belying futurity's vitreous ghost status. |
| 0 | On gravel |
| 2 | I run |
| 8 | with your heart soaked in rainwater and snow, |
| 4 | the smell of pine |
| 1 | against |
| 0 | counted miles. |
| 2 | Chandeliers nictitate— |
| 7 | render me highly hypnotizable. All dreams name |
| 0 | your name with my name. |
| 1 | Travelling |
| 9 | companions beneath the vernacular road lead my tongue astray |
| 3 | from disembodied sentences. |
| 8 | I walk along the vacant bridge in violet |
| 5 | coils of dusk smoke that |
| 2 | dusklight can't |
| 1 | coax. |
| 1 | Euphoria |

| | |
|---|---|
| 0 | withdraws like the hornet of our nettled desire. |
| 5 | Won't you gently deceive me? |
| 5 | Won't you mother my hair? |
| 5 | Won't you take my gaze |
| 9 | to maximize your mantra of war and glide muddled |
| 6 | cauliflower above my breastplate to lessen |
| 4 | there being a night? |
| 4 | Tomorrow I want you |
| 6 | to sleep in day's catalogue of |
| 2 | bleached oak |
| 2 | beneath infinite |
| 9 | bougainvillaea. Scarlet conjunctions catch my |
| | thoughts on midnight's wild |
| 4 | protean frontiers—a bildungsroman |
| 8 | autobiographically dressed to deride the metaphor of |
| | my |
| 9 | homoeopathic dose of saintlike logopoeia. |
| | Admonitions from the tongue |
| 5 | to its bride: roof and quivering oesophagus |
| 4 | defensive below the neck |
| 9 | as to give faded things their microaggressive |
| | tendencies toward |
| 3 | mirrors' counterfeit stigmata. |
| 0 | It's my fata morgana to |
| 3 | drench the chalk |
| 8 | of your white carbon collar. Won't you take |
| 1 | dithering |
| 9 | for the word struck like lightning in my capillaries? |
| 6 | In light-drenched warps, desire's illusion triggers |
| 4 | the infancy of the |
| 4 | fugitive denotations of dunes |
| 2 | collapsing, relapsing |

8    as suns convict at face level. Readable landscapes
8    travel back and forth between abysses and ennui
1    unblushingly.
0    I climb
9    to a name that hasn't been chosen, determined by
7    Solomon who wants to divide it into
5    geology or contemplation—halves of
6    an odour—one to stop breathing,
6    the other to lead me uphill
5    where you are teaching me
9    to unsuture the smog from earth's chordata. How long
3    will you remain
3    the length of
4    my destiny? How does
4    the abacus of planets
6    invite the unwritten architecture of architraves
1    to
2    rescind their
8    winter voices so as to enter our room
4    without drifting into solemnity?
7    I slip beneath the microscope a collage
5    of you sleeping beside debris.
6    All the eddying qualities can't be
4    letters addressed to spring
8    or the flung arms of the cactus shrouded
2    in holy
3    phantasms of rivers.
3    It goes without
7    saying that nothing here is famous except
8    telephone climbers taking their chances at being
       electrocuted
6    finally unwrapped by volts' furious lanterns.

7    It's Sunday again. I am waiting for

8    luminous plaids of light on the pool floor

3    to seduce you.

1    You

6    saturate the air with cotton limousine

5    peregrinations. A counsel of alarms

2    does backflips

7    into augury's meadow of pussywillow where I

1    camouflage

2    its dividends

0    its cadence of myopia

1    its

9    languishing yellow bodice with defoliated fur
         imported from the

0    untidy jargon of hazard. I have often asked

9    you the obvious: don't you want to recede
         into

1    merciless

4    echoes eons from this

5    doctrine of thin dead garments?

6    Instead, I have wanted to ask

4    would you rupture attention

8    by falling into the bellybutton of a snowflake?

5    In the old days, we

6    ate slowly like we knew how

6    a field of snow ensconces leaves.

9    I know I have been wrong before—even after

2    so much

3    of me has

4    counted the dusk's articulations

6    or known how sky isn't a

0    forest walking on water but a

3    receptacle for immortality.
4    In the fibreless night
8    I have craved the accent mark left on
6    the broken walnut shell of insomnia.
1    Your
0    fingerprints categorizing sweetness and ruin—
4    a breakfast embedded in
5    the lighting of a cigarette.
4    What is that thing
3    that finally makes
2    you betray
6    the silviculture status of your sorrow?
6    Is it true what they say:
4    that nasturtiums denote inkwells
8    denote a direct way to swell up a
2    calligraphic desert?
1    I
3    scull a parabola
3    by sexing gravity
9    from tide pools of dandelions shuttering in grey spring.
3    You eat the
6    weeping willows scaffolding bright green narcissism
0    as a way to dilute
7    a sentence tongued in room's linoleum morning.
2    Last night
6    the sky in cloudy mascara escaped
0    to weep next to a thunderstorm.
2    A cryptogram
4    soaks its indecipherable message
9    in modernity's diagonals—a million words in vitro
         return
1    unobstructedly.

4 In the briefest mudslide
1 objectives
2 flamenco out
7 then inward—bullfighting a dank Negra Consentida
3 to lure history
7 into a histrionic bloodbath with Lorca's homosexual
2 crystal photon
4 electromagnetically composed for an
5 amateur nervous system shimmying electric.
8 "Seize the day" as opposed to "seize the
7 fox glinting into view" (the old terror)
0 is my antidote
0 to belief in your plea drenched in water.
6 I wait for you to surrender,
6 to sound eros in tawny syllables.
0 I wait for you to relinquish
6 the sifting light to the dawn.
3 For this ennui
1 splayed
5 I'll take what is easily
5 taken up by the wind
8 as a way of telling you where my
8 thought's destination resides. I'll scull the air mote-
     like.
1 A
7 static particle hanged in a light beam
4 makes it as if
8 hunger lost my address. I write a letter
8 to a pencil and ask if its penis
1 charts
5 a greyish grey atomic heartbeat.
2 Zigging violet

o   through the membrane of the cypress tree
9   I didn't think to spell my name in wood
2   nor to
o   pulverize the vivid core of
9   my restless pianoforte's hermaphroditic disposition
        for sonic clarity as
6   the curtains across my desire sink
2   languorously beneath
8   the sheltering radiator solacing myriad eiderdowns of
        dust.
2   Take me
9   to the chalk heart of this sunk warm place.
2   Take me
5   to your stark lucullan table.
4   Feed me your augury
o   eye so I can see its nilling haunt.
9   This is my heartbeat recanting its shimmering,
        hallucinatory song
1   to
7   say that mirth water is only for
1   draining.
5   If I find you here
3   the tread of
6   contempt has shifted toward a vaticination
4   and blue newness erupts.
3   The surface of
6   your gaze's volcano hems me in.
7   "Is this what wanting is like?" I
8   pull your gaze into a sudden winter flower
9   where the snowdrift never changes and the sun is
2   glass sugar.
5   The oral tongue of glacial

9   memory runs the rim of our last conversation's
      marsupial

0   ache that drills the proverb "Nước chảy đá mòn."

3   Jaded water's stone

6   I have not forgotten to lift.

0   My hand crosses longevity's brow

0   for to leave a youtan poluo near your

1   comb

1   diffidently

3   as if it

3   is an afterthought's

0   most impeccable pronouncement.

5   Your pious sincerity drips with

3   tiny opal pandiculations

0   as if to suggest that the three interlocking tears you
      surrendered on my pillowcase this morning

5   could resurrect with perfection the

4   gradual sadness that hides

8   in every single thin line and its drawnness

8   and live inside the bodice of my grief.

2   Will you

0   unzip the leather jacket of your night's

4   glass mood and lift

6   the rainwater of your heartache from

6   temerity's languid pond? I'd like to

5   kiss the unibrow of sorrow

2   and supersede

1   this

3   twinned blinking preset.

8   "I'm so sorry your brother died this morning."

4   A silked string extends

1   from

4    my heart to yours

6    with life's short-lived fragrance floating (quivering)

9    an inch above the thread. Land and vertiginous bloom

5    ache all day with the

1    aphids'

9    resilient melody of sapphire, and with it,
        resignedness's awakening.

4    To make lace of

1    misfortune,

5    blushing calvinism scatters unliftable stones

1    on

1    my

6    ability to walk behind today's sudden

0    somnial dystopic agency.

9    Please take me to that edge between despair and

4    the grass's million blades

3    and lay my

3    sorrowed head upon

0    a bed of overripe strawberries

5    to perfume me with fullness.

7    What is lacking has migrated its wingspan

2    and reached

7    into the kidney stone of a lullaby

0    fostering arduous passage into

3    my vocal cords.

6    What is ample has cousined my

5    mirror with the illusion of

7    an onslaught of snakes festooned with memorabilia.

5    Would that I stop memorizing

9    the faltering shadow of the laundry line's solemn
        evacuation.

5    Alas I no longer could.

| | |
|---|---|
| 9 | These poems of your grisled anthology of dragged feet |
| 1 | I |
| 9 | chew. The charcoal of your long song's hushed elegy |
| 5 | is hand-rolled tobacco scented. |
| 3 | An obdurate gust |
| 0 | spits out clusters of |
| 9 | the plummeting rungs of our weathervane as if nothingness |
| 2 | were flame |
| 1 | and |
| 8 | you were timber, an embodiment of "qui n'avance |
| 6 | plus," a log length blown asunder. |
| 1 | I |
| 1 | send |
| 7 | your canteen, your umbrella, your morose mushroom |
| 3 | to my tongue |
| 8 | which requires immediate visitation rights from the social |
| 1 | frenulum |
| 9 | of the lowest gustative hemisphere where your memory resides |
| 3 | adrift and ingested |
| 2 | for prandial |
| 6 | sweeps across the plain of me. |
| 1 | Despondently |
| 1 | such |
| 7 | culinary inadequacy leads my taste buds astray. |
| 9 | Under blue electric stove light I burn the supper |
| 3 | with overwhelming monochromatic |
| 1 | pathos. |
| 0 | The clock is forced to articulate "chacun voit midi à sa porte," |

5    not "midi arrive en violet."

1    Confidentially

1    I

8    distort your easy access to my heirloom eggplants

5    and interrupt your kitchen's landscape.

4    You separate this morbid

8    portal from the nervous pressure of luminescent living

0    objects and my recent floral soporificity

7    and bring with it a lavender afternoon,

4    one that holds hostage

4    the slumber of time.

6    There is agency to an ambush

2    that stalks

3    the garden hose

7    from the hollow of its belly like

9    water. The silent architect of potent soil and
        irrefutable

9    poetry injects the surfacing earth with slow muscled
        life

6    while tracing beetle-based hallucinations over
        consciousness

2    iridescently agleam.

7    What keeps my discoloured feet on grass

4    between dog and wolf

9    as if empyrean poise is canine and can howl

6    is precisely the feasibility of howling

7    that you are the prerequisite firmament of.

3    If I didn't

5    withdraw your voracious dehydration from

1    within

8    the closeted betrothed behemoth that the moth-like
        mouth

| | |
|---|---|
| 8 | uses to make tulle of my latent prayers |
| 5 | I would want you to |
| 7 | shimmy between the dead leaves' delicate vitrines. |
| 5 | You fold your French doors |
| 2 | imperialistically puffed |
| 7 | as if their centre is a pendulum |
| 4 | and catastrophe is swung |
| 8 | and somehow capable of slowing down the tendency |
| 9 | to despaghettify the movement of time into gelatinous voids |
| 1 | and |
| 2 | run them |
| 2 | through a |
| 7 | rinse of suns and send them home |
| 9 | to a lightbulb's epicentric heartbeat with a sharpened needle |
| 3 | dressed as Orion. |
| 8 | I think I've hidden inside of a reindeer |
| 1 | with |
| 8 | my toenails blindfolded with Pantone Blue and been |
| 3 | foiled by the |
| 0 | irises for too many summers. |
| 1 | Buried |
| 1 | in |
| 9 | the silver short-haired loam of a soft grazing body |
| 4 | isn't the boreal casket |
| 9 | of full moons lit with small swells of shadow. |
| 1 | Amnesty |
| 2 | streaks in. |
| 9 | It's the first day of May. I take your |
| 8 | green rose leaves to a hillside's viewer pane |
| 3 | whose lens mulches |

3     non-Platonic shapes. Take

6     the diffident reactive gas to the

7     wavering branches whose faded orange pornographic
        petals

3     reveal a monologue

3     of sudden disturbance

6     —the kind you expect to throb

2     like Art

4     Deco before a gargoyle.

4     I can't tell anyone

0     about the scar that behaves like a portal—

6     its prim defeated antlers like keys

5     discarded on the piano fringe

6     beside the music and wasted stems.

6     And the meadows eunuchized by the

4     fervour of sunk seeds!

3     Starfire mixes marigolds

0     into a slew of blundering suns on stems.

8     Iridescent hydrogen wears its flammable blue bonnets as

6     haute couture installations invisibilized by seasons.

0     Don't you already know the moisture of alpine
        strawberry

2     between teeth?

1     Citrus

3     spell, please undo

9     what Baron von Solemacher has pressed against my
        spine.

4     Each vertebra a fruit

9     I bury into the earth of my charred mouth.

4     I wish that you

6     guided the compass of my hips toward

3     your mood's faucet

9    to release the snapdragons pretending to be verdant
       hydras

5    and let them settle into

2    a funeral.

2    In bed

4    the eyelid of a

7    cactus flower shuts softly in the night.

3    The shuddering sky

7    makes myths of cirrus clouds and paints

1    absentmindedly.

9    If ever I am left amid orchids and dreaming

0    of Mrs. Burns's lemon basil

7    please make me a meal of Monday's

0    transgressive clarity

2    and stupor

1    with

7    Wednesday's lilting intensity and beckoning hand
       revealing

9    that you had loved me photosynthetically three
       summers ago.

8    When I toss the stone to summon phosphorescence

6    your rhombohedral crystals piously chastise me

0    and the moon refuses to cleanse them.

9    With raven-shaped minerals—vast like a lunar
       hairbrush—I

4    realign the trickling ache

3    reassign the spasm

7    to the long throat of the train.

0    I derail overnight beside you in a long coat.

2    Armed factions

7    guide local floral targets for hoodwinked neons.

7    A freighter of muscular yellow moves through

0     a burning rosebush.

5     A shape with fractures, aflame.

3     A figure captured

9     from gliding crowds humiliating plumed walkways
         with wallowing abundance

2     and oral

1     pyrotechnics.

7     An immolation stylized by the incursion of

1     cheer

7     and ebullience burns hostility masquerading as
         fervour

6     into ash piles of dandelions. And

2     suppose I

9     furnace the fumes of bathetic applause until it alludes

3     to clarity, turmoil

1     and

7     hushed tenderness, reticently tossing its indigenous
         hair.

6     Dust names what I can barely

7     smoke through the inhospitable pipe that I

5     burgled from the sunset strip

2     radiant enough

3     to orphan photons

8     into semi-automatic particles of sincerity.
         Electromagnetic madness conditions

4     a parabola of fences.

6     In the evening, I ambulate to

7     the deep peace of the municipal bus

4     and wait for you

8     like a green butterfly atop a green leaf.

1     Evoking

8     a quick analogy to sandcastles in an undertow

4   I quickly apologize to
6   twenty miles of amber ridges like
7   a glacial corral cavity hallucinating aural scorn.
6   The initial pigment of tornadoes is
6   borne into a sudden redolent ambergris.
9   In the evening, you see a wave of gulls
4   aphorized as striking pencils
0   confusing our destinations by drawing thin lines
        between them.
5   Some say these misdirections dressed
1   as
3   God's scribbled notes
2   suddenly rise
0   above sea level, above ground level, above
0   distant mountains, above the stone fruit sun, above
0   the helium medium
5   collapsing to a diamond between
6   the morbid thighs of roaming buffalos.
8   Their heavy faces daydreamed of the city you
1   suffocated
2   undersea. Albeit
7   the archaic form confesses its symmetrical fervour
1   for
4   ceremonial mischief with migration
5   inland wedded to filigreed chrome.
2   An outline
6   of synthetic breakfasts forms a disappearance.
3   My overarching umbrellas
5   unfurl to disrupt your subjectivity
6   and your calcium appetite with divinity.
0   So that at times, you are unable to talk
8   while the strawberries bloom out of your ears.

2    Unilaterally heroic

7    velvet candies house musicians who love to

7    fabricate tempos from the landscapes of ponds.

8    So you understand that to love is to

5    soak inside a peaceful pavlova

7    while an hourglass attempts to re-impregnate its

7    certainty with a million minuscule descending
       spheres.

1    You

3    make the horizon

4    my purpose for wanting.

2    Mitigate orchestras.

7    Hyphenate the kiss on the throat of

5    space between city and ocean.

7    And because I desire nothing more than

7    excess minus the length of ideal meaning

8    there is time for the soft symmetry of

9    axonometric ponds. Risking the construct of our
       thoughts by

6    dividing water with waterlessness and subtracting

0    the label "we"

9    is an oblique soliloquy to sombre solitude. A type

1    of

7    astral projection can be referenced later as

3    half the quadrille.

6    A few weeks after I return

3    to wakefulness I

7    unplant my body in preparation for a

1    straight-edged

7    lustful branding that enslaves my tongue to

8    fragrant brachiopods promising lush valleys and
       mended lungs.

7 I am prepared to measure your seafloor
2 with tenderness.
1 Have
4 your handfuls of quartz
6 taken the bullet train to the
8 galvanic river transparentized by assailments of
    moonlight? Have
4 I taken you to
4 a flotsam of illusion
0 where I strip down this garment
9 as my late winter entry into glacially repeating
    gestures
0 of our lack of intimacy?
1 Undulating
2 gradually into
2 eternal aviaries,
4 have you granulated my
9 scarred vowels, barely a thousand, meticulously
    stitched into dimensions
5 worthy of your lexical persuasions?
3 And what will
4 it take for volition
3 to wed itself
0 to the seventeenth-century concept of
1 owning
4 bonnets while surviving? The
6 way the sea has been altered
5 for gilled species on motorcycles
4 riding the chemical highway
9 of flotsam, plastic, synthetic debris, sea-torn nylon,
    oiled salt
5 is by infinitely folding time.

8   You tell me it'd take my body to

5   uncover the nation's opaque plans

3   to infinitely love

7   the calligraphic purple veins of dead gods

1   while

0   occasioning surrealist murders.

5   You take pains to draw

0   impressionistic wounds on deaf husks of corn.

7   From the long bucolic road a young

9   tormented civility enters as a janitor to a labyrinth

2   washing our

2   declarations' underarms.

7   With venerated parsleys, basils, rosemaries dressed in

9   oil sprung from a stone stabbed by sad Athena

6   my body is adorned, healed. My

8   bankruptcy proliferates before the maze is closed
        down.

9   It's a known fact that I do wander endlessly

2   with ceremony.

5   I am a young king

8   without vehicle or cherry blossoms, with unsubsiding
        guilt.

9   My appointment with immortality ceased to exist the
        day

2   my ennui

3   followed me home

5   with champagne in its hand.

4   My frizz is neutral

2   and wry

0   when I watch my champagne glass out-sparkle my
        chandelier

1   and

9    I have no choice but to extend a hiketeria

9    in order to understand the unfortunate accident that
       made

5    my desire for you obsolete.

6    May the branch be privately beheld

1    near

1    your

2    stale mimosa

1    tickling

2    intermittently between

9    the left and right furrows of your statuesque brow.

0    You renew the confidential relic

2    with multiple

1    bastions

9    of definite articles, each seeking to tell the truth

6    about my nocturnal lunar visit with

0    your third-person pronoun.

8    I am king but my gender is not

6    in the scope of your parentheses

4    nor in the horoscopic

0    predilections for nights of gloss.

3    Say I drift

4    among your jingoistic constellates

4    and your adjectives refuse

1    to

8    chant with my bed of anemones, larkspur and

1    parhelia.

5    How my sorrow walks with

9    these sun dogs of shame and spiked violet longing

8    which I have confused belatedly for your need

1    to

3    release me into

6    the unspecified wilderness of your latest

2    obsession with

9    fishing out the splinter that has swelled sky's skin.

7    Again I have mistaken the wound for

7    empirical noise summoning tornadoes of late
        summer.

4    In your basement I

7    coat each nook's darkness with a serum

7    mass-produced by a blind and deaf oracle

1    who

3    wanted to change

0    each of your verbs into a question

9    and your apple-scented prepositions into lazy
        concubines worthy of

9    parading across the baroque halls of your manifold
        sentences.

6    I am in constricted tears from

0    the blue lacuna of weathered skies

5    where pluvial things become parasolic

1    like

8    the gender pronouns of my opening to your

7    sputtering memorial. Yes, everything there was fake

0    and quick to sackcloth

7    our precipitous descent into semi-aquatic undulating
        forests.

2    I am

1    duck-billed

1    and

3    torn in silk

4    and you are the

9    loquacious concubine sipping finality without
        dreaming of Coney Island

9    loquacious concubine sipping finality without
       exfoliating my cathedral face
9    loquacious concubine vajazzling the primitive child
       of my ego
9    loquacious concubine vajazzling time with quartz
       crystals and words
9    loquacious concubine hydrocarboning my pillow
       book in liquid amnesia
9    loquacious concubine hydrocarboning the teeth of
       my small dog.
8    The one who exfoliates my libido without taking
3    my barbed admonitions
7    as a direct expression of my ardent
2    need to
9    refrain from walking my uterus and hippocampus to a
7    wrinkling river with a gold gleaming tooth
8    taped to my pelvis like a micro-gun on
0    a mirror accumulates images.
4    On the back of
9    my tongue there are fictions and dancing purple
       spines.
9    There is also your spit doing backflips and
       somersaults
5    and singing our lazy fortune
1    off-key.
0    It begins with my anguished hippocampus
5    aggressively drawing my neurons outside
9    of the drifting, moaning, hidden, salacious, Oedipal
       night fog
7    in Carl Jung's waistcoat and beneath the
3    library's mockingbird call.
1    I

7   philosophize the denser mass of your animalian
3   concept of solitude:
2   a delta
8   materializes her Greek alphabet as a cancroid way
1   to
6   readjust her canonical method of recanting
0   her solitude as vomited salt water.
9   I suppose it's reasonable to assume that my love
6   is less silent than a plane
3   travelling backward into
1   flames.
8   I suppose it's within reason to reassure you
5   that this ridge is haphazard
9   and that we wouldn't know our way back to
5   offshoots from the ordinary path—
0   the one where my shoelaces billow
2   tentacularly and
4   spectacularly on cue with
4   the tree's summer whips.
5   As your monobrowed eyelashes detach
9   into skinny neighbours caught in an identical
     swelling storm
4   my curling iron makes
5   tidal waves of your hair.
5   Publicly mocking my modest sensibility
3   once again I
4   live without knowing the
6   constant drumming was actually a boat.
9   What does this say about my sonic outlook on
0   the poor quality of your sleep?
8   What does this say about my relationship with
3   infinite plastics dispersing

| | |
|---|---|
| 0 | microscopically inside the uterine wall of |
| 2 | water's figurines? |
| 6 | And what does this say about |
| 4 | your Cadillac of hate |
| 2 | and my |
| 5 | elevator doors to its throat |
| 2 | coughing, lacquered |
| 2 | with bathos? |
| 3 | I am a |
| 0 | lobby in an inert state |
| 8 | waiting for the surgeon of hydrophobic pathology to |
| 2 | enamel my |
| 5 | silhouette and to incise an |
| 3 | anti-intimate sizable frontispiece. |
| 3 | The garrulous nurse |
| 4 | weighs heavily on my |
| 4 | subconsciousness, searing my temple |
| 6 | with unrepeatable conventions only slightly masked |
| 8 | slightly conventional, slightly colourless, slightly chronic, slightly camouflaged |
| 5 | and all this near to |
| 0 | a wild |
| 3 | heart made concrete |
| 5 | by an incorrigible insult and |
| 2 | its detritus. |
| 6 | A penguin sits on an igloo |
| 1 | thinking |
| 9 | that Rodin shouldn't have hired Rilke to be his |
| 3 | sculpture's peeling belfry |
| 1 | nor |
| 1 | his |

| | |
|---|---|
| 8 | secretary, his muse, his man-mistress, his social distress, |
| 8 | his silent friend of many distances, letting himself |
| 1 | paint |
| 7 | silver nails onto the hands of his |
| 1 | orangutan. |
| 0 | Rather, he should have hired the orangutan to |
| 1 | limn |
| 0 | his sculpture's limbs with the effect of early nineties CGI |
| 0 | his maid's aboriginal saliva on Rilke's avatar thighs |
| 0 | his prospector's beard with a wealth of dribbling ale. |
| 3 | It goes without |
| 1 | saying |
| 3 | that certain friendships |
| 7 | are gilded and blessed before they even |
| 8 | relish the coeval pigment of the times that |
| 3 | multiplies their meaning |
| 8 | into quantum materials already pre-made for Breton's outrageous |
| 7 | cow eye slit wide and still seeing. |
| 5 | Art—surrealistic art—is a |
| 2 | limitation and |
| 8 | an imminent request to deny realism's uptight conquest |
| 8 | of the absolute mundanity of your perennial ablutions. |
| 6 | Your shortness of breath I won't |
| 5 | chalk up to the difficulty |
| 8 | of an unforeseen outburst dressed for obstinate occasions. |
| 7 | Stillness trickles gracefully off your velveteen couch. |

| | |
|---|---|
| 5 | Your avuncular rabbit still harbours |
| 3 | a penchant for |
| 3 | my blue carrot-shaped |
| 2 | Rodin sculpture. |
| 0 | It repulses me to find myself ambulating in circles around Lake Mead for nearly thirty hours |
| 8 | rabbitless and without sculpture save for the irregular |
| 3 | bulging bull-baiting burglars |
| 8 | disguised in red cloaks and lumped against twilight. |
| 1 | I |
| 4 | can no longer perambulate |
| 2 | into your |
| 0 | long grey hair |
| 6 | where old men engage in kaffeeklatsch |
| 1 | toasting |
| 7 | their senile smiles against sparkling glasses of |
| 1 | monarchic |
| 7 | ecstasy. The past is unable to reminisce |
| 7 | nor make the appropriate broth for its |
| 6 | brothel's neural-pathway toward the ocean's foamy |
| 6 | mispours. Why haven't you eaten the |
| 9 | thimble-shaped raspberries that I left unthumbed, prewashed on your |
| 1 | visceral |
| 4 | occipital lobe as a |
| 7 | pyramidal gift mimicking our mutually dreamed-of metropolis? |
| 3 | My motor skills |
| 0 | are as imperfect as a foal in sand |
| 3 | but whetted as |
| 5 | fossilized incisors deep in loam. |
| 9 | I don't expect you to eat what I am unable |

| | |
|---|---|
| 8 | to masticate into pristine consistencies and |
| | regurgitate for |
| 2 | the machine |
| 5 | who keeps writing my name |
| 3 | in octopus ink |
| 4 | all over your floor. |
| 9 | That which you mistook for an insult is an |
| o | affront to your thirsty immortality. |
| 4 | I do not expect |
| 2 | you to |
| 8 | love me with both of your eyes open |
| 7 | without seeing my sprawling insatiable aquatic |
| | scrawl. |
| 5 | I know I am hideous |
| 5 | in uncertain weather and beneath |
| 4 | this repugnantly pulchritudinous facade |
| 6 | but I know you are too |
| 8 | forgiving toward blindfolded sylphs who have been |
| | abbreviated |
| 7 | by hip mythologies and interdisciplinary post- |
| | postmodern dissertations. |
| 3 | You dare to |
| I | expound |
| I | defiantly |
| 5 | on all sex as self-care |
| 9 | and on false intimacy as a nomadic device to |
| 5 | navigate me through your door. |
| 6 | With nerve-wracking Buddhism, I will censor |
| 2 | monomaniacal lust |
| 8 | as an antidote to flawed enlightenment dressed as |
| 6 | day and night chain-smoking each other. |
| 3 | I am here |

| | |
|---|---|
| 8 | in the midst of the twilight's varicose veins |
| 8 | and bullet wounds. Imbibing through a saxophone-shaped straw |
| 2 | are the |
| 3 | pink purgatories of |
| 5 | each under the weather newborn. |
| 3 | In response to |
| 7 | your pestering implicit question, I have never |
| 8 | actually slept under your duvet of soiled metaphors |
| 7 | your dishonest comforter of weird lies your |
| 5 | tear-soaked pillow cases of entrapment. |
| 9 | I hoist my thoughts barely six inches off the |
| 3 | ground. I insist |
| 7 | that you, the child of a masqued |
| 5 | ball, bathe me in almond |
| 1 | shaped |
| 9 | pine nuts to provoke confusion, upheaval, and skepticism to |
| 5 | the hundredth degree. I would |
| 7 | never make you love me without resorting |
| 7 | to my sultriest tactics to unfurl umbrellas. |
| 8 | Standing under the yellow parasol, I measure the |
| 1 | breadth |
| 8 | and monsoon season of the umbrellas' clandestine relationship |
| 5 | to mycelium desiring garbage cylinders. |
| 7 | I toss the parasol aside and allow |
| 7 | the mathematician to describe Saturn's moonlet miles. |
| 8 | She inspects the numerical values of the lunar |
| 0 | psalm book, each song sprouting |
| 5 | meteorites the size of twenty |
| 3 | acre apple farms. |

2    Each capable

1    of

7    hiding immigrants in oyster shells and apple

1    barrels.

2    With large

2    promises, you

6    appear too similar to suppressed similes

8    to be anything but a comparison to truth.

0    After standing alone without that yellow parasol, I bend down to

6    pick the softest flowers. I bend

6    to remove one errant hair from

1    your

3    blue ostrich's eyelid

0    that closes delicately as starvation.

0    I know you don't think that soft flowers can think for themselves, but

1    motion

9    is a metaphor for still life that harbours resentment.

2    Any movement

7    without motion is overrated and best left

8    to Parrhasius and his painting of a curtain.

7    I design windowless meadows and pre-dawn hues

6    to compete with the swilling day.

6    I collect your voice in a

1    wentletrap

1    wentletrap

1    wentletrap

9    and it distils my soul like French wine in

5    your small and perfect mouth.

9    When sadness visits me in her long evening gown

0    I am in my best bonnet, applying

9 my prenuptial moisturizers before being cloaked in
timeless white

2 moon dust.

1 The

6 eighty-two moons of Saturn are listing

4 their hydrogen-rich sexual preference

2 for chemistry

0 and are rewriting their lunar personal ads.

1 Hawk

9 for helium delirium in the right place. At the

8 right moment in which you undress your ambush

9 I will deflower an ancient vase by smashing it.

3 I hurry forward

8 without gazing back at you for assurance and

0 slip on a slick dash of tile.

9 My desire has been sitting on a chair facing

5 Neptune's scopophilic moons and I

2 yearn to

5 hurl myself there from afar.

7 By nature not hubristic, you turn my

2 waning gibbous

0 earlobes away from your megaphone

1 saying

0 "I hope the leafy voice of the air has woken up to sing
for you"

6 and "Today is crisp like lettuce."

5 You say, "Bikini i ull."

4 I want one for

8 my Norwegian flight into woollen woods waiting in

5 the mailbox outside my door.

8 Dying, my brother prewashes the head of a

6 lunar cabbage whose pale prosodic folds

3     remind him of

2     wave crests.

7     He wallflowers his urge to dismiss the

8     desire of gravity to make everything into spheres—

8     ones that could prophesize the biblical momentum of

6     a dragon salivating over a newborn.

5     King Solomon at one point

9     regretted his wisdom and sewed the child back
           together.

3     His mother(s) were

6     also regretful for having asked Solomon

1     to

5     answer any question at all.

3     I suppose time

3     has sliced us

8     biblically speaking into quadrants instead of halves
           and

1     refuses

8     to ascertain possessive mothers who prefer to recede

2     nyctinastically like

7     Cinderella's slipper dipped in pale semi-nyctophobic
           ice.

9     Time waits under a tree of ommatophilic birds with

6     bloodlust for in-flight salted pretzels baked

8     in hot engines propelling you over geometrical
           expanses.

2     I love

3     appearing in your

0     periodic table

3     as a rainbow.

0     There are obvious things in it such as Ethereum
           dressed like Bitcoin

1    permeating

9    as consciousness without consciousness. Derision
       holds an inlet for

5    funnelling your disrobed antique valuables

2    so that

0    they might know the seaside

3    as divided into

5    salt air and seagull laughter.

3    Drawn across the

0    ripples in the wet sand closest to the pawing ocean

1    I

8    can't remember if we called it philosophy or

5    bionic miscommunication or floral admiration.

2    But I

9    am a huge believer in digital currencies that bark

6    at the harried protestors who answer

8    to wizened denizens who shave only 34% of

9    their heads so as to access a god. Who

9    is the number one gynaecologist of a vision for

5    the dappled and undappled things?

7    And who the seventh psychoanalyst of Bourdain's

7    blue hotel room of sorrow before he

3    committed his soul

6    to the colour of oyster shells?

2    A culinary

2    violet conchology

5    concocts the nearly quiet estuary

9    in which are buried the tiny bones of quail.

9    In the eardrums of your sister's Hello Kitty backpack

4    which is a hive

1    sedated

3    by exquisite poisons

8    is conched the hexagonal toxin created to suppress

9    the zodiac's heterologies with my expressions over
          last breakfast.

1    It

2    dismays me

4    that you are so

9    benevolent toward the inner melody of snails who don't

7    join the Church of Jesus Christ of

2    Proterozoic Saints

1    impulsively

7    to save souls, eddies on their backs.

7    When I dip my oiled head into

5    God's sudden pond of tears

2    Eve reappears

8    holding out each of her ribs, which bloom

3    like Cai Guo-Qiang.

4    I love the taste

7    of his gunpowdered fireworks on my tongue

9    their mineral detritus settling like sharp stones. In the

1    obsolescent

3    gaze of adolescence

1    on

5    the ripeness of a swamp

1    I

5    lay tall dry grass over

5    God's bald head. As a

7    slick baby parrot, I need to feed

4    on blue cumin seeds

8    and be perfumed with a hundred reasons to

5    slander the colour yellow and

7    send its bobbing tulips to the pound.

2    As a

4   hound foaming at the

2   impotent edge

4   of my crystalline sanity

5   I can easily recreate the

4   hound dog's pound sound.

1   I

5   set my howl toward the

0   primate's convexed blindness whose expansive lack of civility

6   decorates the theatre of my monstera.

9   A despondent recollection of my chthonic time with Beatrice's

5   illustrious and physical swimming pools

9   becomes purgatory. On its ninth path, it still couldn't

5   chlorinate accurately, green my hair

0   in such a way that when God recreates genesis for the second time, he would be inspired to change his gender pronoun to

8   that of a seedling entering the verdant Chthulucene.

2   As a

9   vast army of metabolic newness sinks through God's skin

5   Elon Musk's silent leaf blower

3   scooches its astral

3   bedrock nonbinary androgyny

1   into

1   steric

6   groupings like covens of fish eggs.

8   There is a time for darkness and there

6   is a time for darkness's punctum.

1   You

7 misunderstand the alignment of our associative
   wounds

2 and I

7 can hardly stop forgiving you for it.

8 As a result, my salad days have been

5 brimming with meringues of lovingkindness.

5 Thistle-loving goldfinches pinched by the

8 conical morning call into my gaping netted window.

8 I take this as a prophetic sign of

9 the future personality of your daydreams, which
   hover endlessly

0 above the liminal space between your candleblower and

7 its hairdryer. They send your mechanical breath

5 pungent with chocolate chip cookies

0 into our late oven's memory of a bygone era.

9 It is this nostalgic preconditioned outpour of a redolent

8 array of dead flowers hung on the doorknob

3 that you changed

8 when you gave up dying's explicit beseeming ornaments

1 to

7 the space between the balcony and grave.

5 In the afterlife I banish

4 your preference for cauliflower

6 and your preference for boiled broccoli

3 and your preference

7 to keep me in a goldfinch's cage

4 to the ninth circle.

6 I still won't forgive you for

4 dipping my supper in

9 your hermaphroditic basin meant for my nocturnal
   urinal disposal

3 so you could

| | |
|---|---|
| 9 | water the neophytal hyacinths that had just spent their |
| 3 | best years learning |
| 1 | to |
| 9 | etch their Palestinian azure into the shape of grief. |
| 2 | An ex-Zionistic |
| 5 | blooming cries thirteen storeys high |
| 5 | while self-euthanistic bombs explode in |
| 0 | the embryos of tulip bulbs and the uteri of dolphins. |
| 6 | The aftermath of this religious war |
| 0 | settles into born and aging beings— |
| 4 | ones that attack the |
| 0 | tulip hearts of dolphins |
| 0 | and the Shoah's desire to end all potentially slow-moving, slow-growing genocidal carnage. |
| 9 | In the second Eden I ask for five red |
| 2 | monarch butterflies |
| 7 | to make a headdress for my snake. |
| 7 | I also ask for nineteen wives who |
| 0 | will sour your endless geometries with |
| 1 | their |
| 6 | sisterly countability and thin delicate wrists |
| 7 | and who will take turns taking Eve's |
| 1 | finesse |
| 1 | down |
| 3 | a notch or |
| 9 | two. Your inevitable hydraulic thirst for sadomasochistic sexual pairings |
| 0 | of plants and insects and inventions of female moths without mouths |
| 0 | won't be deprived of their monotheistic |
| 9 | thoughts as they lay themselves under the weight of |
| 8 | God's master plan to keep earth's inmates ontologically |

4   "singular" like a tongue

8   twisted into one of Zeno's paradoxes. To exclude

8   motion as a mode of being a cyclone

2   is like

4   saying there's no easy

0   way treat God's autism, his Asperger's syndrome,
      when he impulsively tweets about his DOGE's
      wayward disciples and his pseudo-hustling
      techniques to reinvent the second Eden

1   as

2   "hospitable Mars."

8   Its rivers will need refilling with perhaps juice

5   squeezed from two hybrid-grapefruits, three

8   pomelos turned inside-out, and four Meyer lemons
      from

3   Greenland, Australia, and

6   a penguin huddle's centre in Antarctica.

1   I

6   don't blame you for wanting to

0   remove all the unblown birthday candles from a
      funnel cake baked by

3   a cold penguin

5   and I don't blame you

6   for then blowing them all out

3   without wearing your

7   latest letter's sorrowful limping tone as a

0   triangular hat

7   patterned with a planetary darkness in expansion.

6   But I will blame you for

6   drawing the shape of huddled penguins

0   as a square when it should be the shape of

1   cleptobiosis

| | |
|---|---|
| 0 | and the colour of Cambodian red. |
| 4 | Oh we can smoke |
| 7 | without a solar panel, pretending to be |
| 1 | righteous |
| 0 | and obnoxiously patient |
| 1 | like |
| 8 | a pre-used and pre-measured "vintage" tablespoon's silvery back. |
| 1 | I |
| 9 | have come to cherish my time in second Eden |
| 4 | since God has been |
| 2 | on the |
| 9 | cusp of filling its rivers and conjuring its seedlings |
| 5 | with oral sex made generic |
| 5 | as an infinitely reproducible spectacle. |
| 5 | Even retinal pleasure feels jealous! |
| 9 | I have come to loathe my time in second |
| 6 | Eden because you have hyper-linked my |
| 1 | heart |
| 9 | to a poorly pruned rhodochiton near Adam's left foot |
| 8 | and I know it is there to stay. |
| 9 | Two opposing hearts separated by a despondent biblical narrative |
| 4 | coalesce in fountain shapes. |
| 6 | On the eighth day, God video-chatted |
| 7 | with the shape of a fountain so |
| 6 | a liquid conversation could musically condense |
| 7 | a blue hive at your ear's centre. |
| 8 | God closes his eyes and his laptop simultaneously. |
| 3 | Heads to bed. |
| 7 | He questions his recent sour relationship with |
| 4 | China's rabbiting Yutu-2 rover. |

4   If only he had

9   swatted it from the moon who he believes is

4   too effeminate, too maritally

4   attached to far-off tides.

8   Lunar waves have conspicuous menstrual cycles too
      cyclical

2   to master

5   without, apparently, heavily taxing tampons.

5   What has always been necessary

3   won't survive to

7   announce my latest heart-shaped bloom. Time's ugly

9   green hands have been made and designed to
      annihilate

7   space's most remarkable hairdos with constant
      retouching.

7   Time's ogling of the camel's searing eye

4   at the heart of

7   Adam's retractable redemption is the psychological
      urgency

2   that fondles

6   Eve's left breast and notices that

8   it is the exact weight of a jar

4   filled with overripe strawberries.

7   He cannot help but make jam with

1   her

0   and then toast to spread it on.

4   Lucifer's elongated ophidian bodice

0   so entrances him that he is compelled to write the
      Bible's palinode

4   without touching his left

7   toast staling in the new knowledgeable sun.

5   Eve, meanwhile, reaches for her

| | |
|---|---|
| 3 | strawberry breast, so |
| 4 | brightly crimson, seed-studded, she |
| 6 | completely forgets both good and evil |
| 4 | and changes the palimpsest |
| 6 | of God's journal and chokes on |
| 2 | pages and |
| 0 | pages of judgement. Deep beneath dust bunnies are |
| 8 | ravines of ennui seeking Moses' trimmable beard for |
| 0 | roses and oiling, making Aaron jealous. Moses' robes are yet unspattered, |
| 4 | his brotherhood anaesthetized against |
| 6 | the few remaining locusts who drift |
| 6 | like ugly nymphs pontificating on an |
| 8 | unlost bet that magnetized their world to wrinkled |
| 4 | insomnia. God, after being |
| 2 | difficult, climbed |
| 5 | onto Magdalene's scrawny left shoulder |
| 9 | to whisper that her perfume was still intact and |
| 0 | if she doesn't mind, could she bottle her post-prayer sweat to be used as holy water |
| 6 | with which to drown the locusts |
| 9 | who were too eager to fornicate in the millions |
| 4 | and so reflect everything. |
| 9 | As a fraudulent federal ecological disaster, an insurance scam |
| I | spangles |
| 2 | cancel culture |
| 9 | into the ephemeral world with its caught open mouth. |
| 3 | Cumin accentuates our |
| 3 | intimacy's ruse, masquerading |
| I | as |
| 3 | a roughed gust. |

6    The crucifix reveals the mouths of

7    shadows to be located at its intersection.

7    God isn't the kind of holy ghost

0    to make stones out of bread and hail them from the
        sky without prompting, without being "aggressed"

2    without undulating

8    between types of pills making gusts' voices fainter

9    and zephyrs' echoes abandoned sonic asymptotes. Yet
        there is

8    no telling when I was thrust into the

9    oblivion that you audaciously call "Diego Rivera's
        post-apocalyptic mural"

1    orchestrating

5    Kahlo's violent pelvic pain as

2    free maps

1    outlining

0    bionic anguish as a mode of ascension.

4    Faunal sensation and mystic

7    days of discipline will break your leg.

5    Underneath thirty thousand heads of

2    lettuce, I

1    defy

6    the offer you could not refuse.

2    At least

0    put yourself on the phone as a confirmation of exile

5    or a neon green cocktail

6    will ignite my mown heartbroken lawn.

9    Below a low ceiling of ignitable desire I clandestinely

6    plummet into the ground's emerging mouth

6    while sexual caterpillars and legless zeros

0    annihilate the sky's potential to grin—

2    lips striating

4     into curled drowning canticles.

o     Esoteric agencies lead hyaloid insects

5     into iridescent hallucinations of dew.

8     There are dream landscapes within dream landscapes bivouacking

o     so as to avoid the city's hurried slumber.

3     Colourblind the outfield

8     with brilliant orange pop flies from outer space!

1     Denote

5     collisions of your loose moons!

o     Denote

1     kaleidoscopes

9     mocking polychromatic aubades like they belong to a Shakespearean

3     trio of daughters!

5     I suppose when God manufactured

1     logomania

1     he

2     wung presence

5     metre by metre. Exquisitely our

3     future wrongs dress

3     in repellant horizons

8     disguised as blue Cadillacs and disperse in electric

2     mnemonic magnesium.

4     So as to undo

3     infinity one number

o     at a time and spin it into a very fine thread

o     we cut particles of whispers into a million pieces

3     and speak into

5     a megaphone designed for cubic

5     understandings of time and space.

8     I squeeze between abdominal layers of betrayal and

| | |
|---|---|
| 7 | miscommunicate through what I still hear as |
| 6 | your insincerity refining and clamouring your |
| 4 | opulent flight to San |
| 0 | Diego. A stampede, a staircase |
| 2 | a slant |
| 4 | a sling shot through |
| 7 | seventeen extra reasons to have "really tried." |
| 4 | To provoke a grasshopper |
| 9 | is also to rise like a sun or locomotive. |
| 6 | From the outer post, your lingerie |
| 4 | shimmers like a flag |
| 7 | and makes me love your bras even |
| 3 | more than I |
| 2 | love the |
| 6 | folds of your skirt rippling against |
| 3 | the axial diphthong |
| 9 | of your ankle bone presiding above your forgotten shoe. |
| 1 | I |
| 4 | hesitate in front of |
| 1 | a |
| 9 | serpent of wind ruffling the baroque anxious palm tree |
| 9 | as if my navy blue dildo strap-on heavily depends |
| 2 | on your |
| 7 | willingness. To casually deny my salty orache |
| 2 | and croon |
| 6 | through the orange grove that is |
| 0 | the orache's subconscious |
| 4 | approach to a bellyache |
| 2 | spells doom |
| 6 | for foreplay. Spells of unsatisfying Sisyphean |

9     doom's like forever painting and unpainting Eros'
        chewed nails

9     with multichromic nail polish invented by Psyche's
        incorrigible brother-in-law.

2     She didn't

2     greenscreen his

7     implacable backdrops of books by women authors

9     so an impercipient librarian who uses too much
        moisturizer

6     instead of seeing these intellectual tomes

7     as organ donations for patients with illiteracy

8     will see the wayward lime green photons justify

2     their pre-existing

3     biblical errancy. Masquerading

5     as the backdoor to celestial

4     cabbage folds of time

7     are two transhumeral amputees plucking an oboe.

8     They plait the air with severed music carrying

1     amnesia

6     and so fill us with forgetfulness

3     and morning sadness.

## Caina's Complaint

6    When Cain became a strict vegetarian

0    Abel started butchering two young goats.

0    Because he saw death as as impressive gift, he made

9    an oblation much desired by God and his unrivalled

3    penchant for ablutions.

4    Separating the vegetables from

1    flesh

7    Cain turned to God and said bitterly

2    "Why can't

1    you

6    appreciate a zucchini's thin velvet movement?

4    Life is too short

1    to

2    have a

1    tantrumic

9    relationship with summer squash. Life is too short
        to

9    spend less than an eon outside the shelter of

2    huddled cauliflowers

4    Gregorian chanting to soil.

5    I know we don't see

8    the secret language of roots spreading cursively in

6    my verdant sacrifice for your irrational

3    preference for light.

1    I

5    don't blame you. It doesn't

0    give me pleasure knowing that while I compete for
        your acceptance and attention, my wilted carrots

3    nestle eternity in

0    radiant anticipation

2   of your

8   body odour secreting at 1.2 gallons per second.

6   Yes, that they will be reinvigorated

1   by

8   their proximity to your scent's ample royal folds.

2   I wrap

9   myself around a lemon's body like an imperfect
      translation

7   of my mother's profound thirst to demobilize

4   the eggplant's sex life.

5   Disband my zucchinis from purgatory!

5   Deter my radishes from pigment!

5   Protect my okras from slippage!

7   Settle my uniform-embedded rows of fallow sorrow

0   so the rosebush doesn't grow emotionally hungry

6   and the aphids shall invent lace

7   to combat your dense cacological addiction

4   and requests for newness!

9   If the role were reversed, Father—meaning, if I

8   sang to you in secret and called you

3   AMC short squeeze—

8   I would cut a door into your hillside

5   and plant a willow tree

0   in its threshold. I'd hold the cut door open, as wide as
      possible

5   so that wool and fibre

4   would be your fortresses

9   and my inability to succumb to your semifinal
      appearance

4   would slip off like

5   mascara from an oily, glassy

8   replaceable eye in the head of an archive.

8    It's time, Father, to address your irrational
          favouritism
5    toward music that is practised
8    too intensely by Eve when she tries cannabis
6    and indents time with love of
9    portable dispensaries. When I killed my beloved
          brother without
2    flutes or
6    rage, you were passive-aggressively seething and
9    pressed the air to spheres like a dropped alka-seltzer.
9    I wish you weren't so fixatingly binary about how
5    wind pushes trees' hair back
6    as if hair could resolve the
9    rift between our mothers who banter eloquently at the
0    aqueducts. All the rivers of misfortune
9    tie themselves in a violent knot like dreams turned
2    Jung-dormant, Akhtar-rooted,
7    fussy as the skirts tutuing the mountains
2    as plateaus.
1    To
0    relinquish chance over fate
7    and settle into a new hill I
9    teach myself how to speak knoll-language, the kind that
7    turns to a balm when it slips
5    and pinky-swears with square roots
0    and bends the hypotenuse so it sings like a violin
          string.
9    Father, there would be no first murder if I
3    was born in
0    a biometric bath
2    outside anarchy.
9    I wouldn't lose my olive branch, my mind, my

| 5 | compos mentis when Eve plays |
| 5 | John Cage's 4'33" in less |
| 3 | than one minute. |
| 2 | As forty |
| 1 | rounds |
| 1 | seconds |
| 6 | later are fired with glee by |
| 5 | Adam's catcalling of wild geese |
| 3 | they uniformly honk. |
| 4 | As the apple wilts |
| 4 | digesting in the snake |
| 9 | our afternoon is limned by tan lines and drawn-out |
| 8 | poolside conversations about slimming tea and the nature |
| 7 | of Eve's unorganized reproductive organs. Indeed, the |
| 2 | Satanic horns |
| 0 | were painted and unpainted overnight by Hieronymus Bosch who had to time-travel from fifteenth century's Hertogenbosch to find |
| 2 | bistre and |
| 7 | liver pain as ideal pigments with which |
| 5 | to depict the human shape |
| 5 | to depict the ophiolitic sin |
| 9 | to depict the semi-white equilibrium of moonlight in tunnels. |
| 6 | Father, don't you think I have |
| 0 | gained instant fame in knowing at least the names of all things? |
| 2 | Father, don't |
| 3 | consult local dignitaries |
| 6 | about our dilapidated apple orchard when |
| 4 | you know perfectly well |

8    that my sisters wanted very much a second

o    puppy so that you would finally articulate emotion

6    in a way that isn't shameful.

6    You call them 'angel girls' like

5    they are the original actresses

4    of your Hollywood romances.

9    After all, this is their second opportunity to re-sin

9    and finally swat away your plethora of virtuous
        trumpets.

1    This

1    might

9    explain why I took my daughters into the forbidden

8    'as seen on TV' shopping networks to sell

8    aluminum and copper salad spinners to the
        Kardashians

1    who

8    happily and unabashedly showcase their post-surgical
        pointy cleavage.

3    Such round glistenings

4    of silicone, of saline

7    bobbing atmospheric moons in a pool!

9    I could easily eat these lunar materials like gummy

7    bears. I could make up an excuse

7    that I had confused the night for

5    a confectionary feast or an

3    apricotic refusal to

5    select just one only, since

6    feasting might have many doors but

6    never more than one chamber window

3    at a time.

6    And so I find myself where

9    Bitcoin has bitten my ass. The crypto market has

8    shut its jaws softly over the entire body

o    of fiat-culture, fiat-institutions, of it-shall-be culture!
       Of let-it-be-done culture! Fiat! Fiat! Such

7    lordly declarations make us miss naming animals.

4    When I walk backward

2    into dense

6    cumulus clouds, I imagine you forgiving

5    my ankle bones for breaking

4    my brother's neck into

2    small morsels

5    of vestigial light—ones buried

2    deep within

7    the Terracotta Armies of Qin Shi Huang

8    and in the flaming hearts of burning books.

6    But I was too ambitious to

2    resculpt the

5    architecture of your merciless imprecation

5    and douse it with five

I    zany

8    herbs and add garlic so as to banish

I    desire

8    from entering my doorstep and settling in my

4    fish bowl shaped heart.

I    I

7    forgive you, Father, for banishing me to

5    wander your rows of vegetables

7    and your infinite labyrinths of guilt entanglements.

4    They cordon around my

6    sacral chakra like Lucifer's onerous tail

7    swatting back and forth to fan the

2    boiled saucepan

8    of all your favourite breakfast foods such that

9   the charcoal smoke can disguise the irreverent
       afterimage of

0   the past thousand years of your hapless,
       commentitious life.

9   Father, where was Mother when I murdered my
       brother?

7   Was she sharing silence with a ripple?

7   Was she grinding favouritism back into salt?

7   Was she flaring desire with a cigarette?

7   Was she berating you for neglecting to

2   stand luminous

7   before my decision to end elite contempts

9   and let things happen as they happen but also

3   to warn you

8   that by murdering my brother I meant 'nothing

0   is nothing.' Sinning is my way of enacting my savage
       authority over

0   your image of me as someone standing in a patch of
       forget-me-nots. As someone

0   with an undeniable will to erase

8   the sound of wind chimes at your window

1   and

6   the potential movement of rubber bands.

4   I live intoxicatingly. Outside

7   you sound your latest refusal to alter

0   the quick decay

6   of my four subterranean fish heads.

0   I suppose your future son had intended to convert
       these (my afflictions that are) into the bread and
       butter of my ethical relapse—though I wouldn't
       have minded the transfiguration of fish heads into
       wine or bread

o   to be divided infinitely among my friends and
            enemies—and yet on these inexhaustible loaves
            do my afflictions also remain spread interminably.
            And so
1   you
6   feast on my churned immoral sorrows
1   and
4   chew it thirty-two times
5   and you expect me to
2   thank you.
4   You diminish the arrow
9   flaming across time to connect me with my kin.
1   Father
9   you are egregiously not amenable to roasted eggplant
            or
2   perhaps you
1   disdain
7   my method of ingeniously crop-rotating my oblation
3   but I reckon
2   sacrifice doesn't
1   tally
7   its fingertips, doesn't distinguish what is bruised
2   from what
1   is
4   running delicate and sweet.
7   I purposefully wait until my labour rots
7   and gives like too lush plums in
2   sedition of
3   your carnivorous mood.
5   How annoyingly unappealing you are
o   in my soul's factory farm swaying among the meat
1   vegan-sedated

| | |
|---|---|
| 4 | and slinging commandments like |
| 1 | you |
| 4 | still possess your skin. |
| 4 | My sin can't rehypothecate |
| 1 | your |
| 9 | infinite, homophobic, preferential treatment for my brother. My illegitimacy |
| 7 | sets me at the edge of your |
| 3 | lake and for |
| 5 | the sake of a question |
| 6 | there is still plenty of room |
| 8 | for the fraught sempiternal daymare of your answers. |
| 5 | I'm trans and female now |
| 4 | as are my sentences. |
| 8 | The male part of me did kill Abel |
| 1 | and |
| 6 | the female in me reveals your |
| 1 | incoherent |
| 3 | distaste for myopic |
| 6 | geniuses like John Keats and also |
| 1 | Sappho |
| 1 | who |
| 5 | teases Li Po relentlessly for |
| 7 | his drunkenness and one thousand poems about |
| 3 | witty Michelle Obama. |
| 5 | Her Portuguese water dog's penchant |
| 2 | for urinating |
| 5 | on the second amendment is |
| 5 | an adamant response to the |
| 2 | misfiring of |
| 1 | dehydrated |
| 3 | conspiracies pertaining to |

3  shorting AMC shares
4  for the cinematic glitterati.
7  The hermaphroditic part of me has not
5  advised me not to ask
7  you zealously about Abel's nonchalant seduction of
4  your Holy palate by
1  zaftig
8  flocks of chickens, lambs, Adaptaurs, honey-bees,
        and seagulls
4  I choose not to
9  sip this particular juice, but rather press the
        grapefruits
4  against my mother's kneecaps
6  and watch the flocks of bees
8  enter the small battlefield of bleeding hearts, orchids,
4  cirsium vulgare and cyclamen
3  whose perennial vultureness
8  swoops down to put into abrupt resolution your
5  manic appetite. To clarify our
2  mother's exclamation,
3  a holy virtue
3  you don't extol
2  Father, you
3  might have taught
9  me how to love my brother in a way
0  that freudenfreudes his jubilant cries. I hierarchize
        my atrophying gestures to quietly admonish
        myself  within
7  the innocent spy hole through which my
3  mother peeks and
9  drop by drop administers her heirloom of rare
        liqueur.

4    With the luminescent beehive

1    you

4    choose with your stomach

3    you repudiate me

3    and relinquish Abel's

3    close reading of

4    sibling rivalry gone awry.

5    Before his blood drained out

4    I watched the trees

7    lose their immortal vision of what was

7    once a willingness to testify. Via the

6    sacred perversion concealed within the forbidden

2    taste of

4    arboreal clairvoyance, I traffick

1    my

6    brother's soul into existence's primary medium.

8    In the green bulb of the bull thistle

6    rests an extremely diminutive version of

2    the marrow

5    of my quiet desire to

1    falteringly

8    diminish Abel's breath. I could've pummelled him
        with

9    your collection of ram horns that I found in

8    your holy basement near Tesla's cybertruck recharge
        station

3    where Abel would

5    sleep overnight with the campfire

6    dwindling to embers by his side.

9    His body heat, his lucent mouth open in the

4    chorus of night voices

8    breaks the sopranic temperature of how much I

| | |
|---|---|
| 5 | thought I loved him. Now |
| 5 | I prefer his inability to |
| 6 | reason with the Father about his |
| 2 | appointment with |
| 0 | the hundred thousand angels with emotional |
| | disorders, how meat had 'cured' them, how their problems had stemmed from nothing other than diet, despite war, irrelevance, dry scalp, polyester, and the like. |
| 9 | Yes, I fanned the cherubic engine of demise until |
| 9 | it willed itself into a lifelong hallucination of fratricide. |
| 2 | Forgive me |
| 1 | for |
| 9 | wanting to replace your body heat with the mistress |
| 2 | selling frozen |
| 2 | dairy daiquiri- |
| 2 | flavoured popsicles |
| 1 | foreign |
| 8 | to most earthlings except those closest to the |
| 4 | extraterrestrial surface of hashtagable |
| 2 | flowers and |
| 7 | skinny dipping bumblebees and crystalized chirosophists lobotomizing |
| 2 | lily pads. |
| 5 | Father, isn't it time for |
| 5 | nightly bouts of gratitude for |
| 0 | your irrational devotion to light? |
| 2 | Isn't it |
| 5 | possible for me to undo |
| 4 | the braid of your |
| 2 | cognitive dissonance |

5   and entwine a ribbon within

6   your conscience's rigorous expediency, which vaguely

8   matches the movement of my mudsliding nefarious
        idea

8   to drag Abel's severed body leisurely, but also

7   to light a cigarette while doing so?

6   Nicotine satisfaction has always been my

7   method of alluring mystique while I devastate

1   your

7   seventeenth-century conception of family, ankles and
        politesse.

9   It's also my innocuous way to wage war against

0   the lungs' questionable holiness (or the firmament's?).
        I can't remember my reasoning exactly, but

4   developing lung cancer is

9   merely a way of isolating the clouds in a

4   category five hurricane drill.

6   It makes it easier to sink

0   sinners in an artificial flood designed to

1   waken

6   a city lost in a miasmal

5   encounter with passing time like

3   it's nothing—or

4   at least less than

6   an ounce of your delicate spit

6   touching the cigarette's succinite spongy lip.

8   Father, don't you want me to love your

0   flora just as much as your fauna, your

4   coral and this correlation

9   just as much as you love the correlates of

8   Humphrey Bogart's vibrant and rustic masculinity
        with the

8 preference for women who love history as told
6 through the backwater of an African
2 Technicolour Queen?
7 I have forgotten how much you want
2 to vacuum
3 my childhood bedroom
2 to water
7 the flaccid, etiolated gazania in my soul's
9 window sill planter box. The only remaining bloom
    now
1 is
7 dust-coloured like my everlasting carpet and its
8 evanescent phoretic, synthetic contours demarcate
    my pervasive abomination
6 objectionable to your eyes only, Father.
0 I have forgotten how much you censor
8 insignias, and pale green bars of soap, modernist
5 approaches to leisure, self-care and
7 shipwrecks that settle into elaborate undersea
    garlands.
8 Aquatic chandeliers give octopi only worthy
    adversaries and
4 rival the whale skeletons!
3 It is time
8 to welcome a couch to your floorboards, Lord.
3 You and I
8 can sit on it even though it is
2 designed to
7 seat only very small accessory dogs and
9 three ice cubes in a jar. Some gallimaufry of
6 impolite instruments incites very soft strumming.
7 If you were my therapist, Father, what

9    would you suggest for corporeal longing, for occult
        signals
7    to release my intense eagerness to slaughter
6    my brethren in a violent sweat
6    to eliminate the fratricidal thought that
8    slowly falls through the blackness of my days.
1    I
4    lengthened the metaphors of
5    my vacant rose in hopes
4    of making buoyant my
1    conviction
0    that rocks are not so porous after all. They won't
        absorb
0    your intense affection for
9    the high winds of forgiveness screaming in the belfry.
5    Your crippling monomania for lucid
3    dreaming bucks against
8    your disagreeable, primitive, boxy method of
        binarizing animals
8    and then further denigrates them in the Great
3    Flood. There, you
7    cluster them into piles of searing skin
8    cluster them into things that give penguins hiccups
6    cluster them into several accidental glances!
3    At one point
6    what was given over to me
0    was the way you divinely gazed at Abel
9    as he cleared your vast table with oven mitts.
5    It seems ridiculous that the
0    rain-filled valleys and vibrating tongues of corn did
        not
6    give you culinary pleasure as much

8    as the delicately seasoned and ice-bathed cow
        tongues.

0    In retaliation for your unfair and unappealing gaze, I
        have been wearing an iron apron

0    and spurs, even holding a lance noctambulously

6    but murdering Abel will take time

4    and corrosive fuchsia meditations."


2    "Cain, I

2    de-poison my

5    garden of scorn and desolation

1    to

2    give you

5    the bite of an aurulent

2    justification for

0    my omnipotence, which is to say I

5    have no excuse for my

1    geriatric

1    prejudice

7    for the coiled shell-like horns of rams.

3    I denied you

9    a New Age diet and free use of Alleppey

2    turmeric in

9    your falafels of self-importance and pitchers of
        golden milk.

8    Cain, the first child of the universe, my

4    fruitarian life is over.

8    Before the great oblation, I knew things between

9    you and Abel were taut as a rubber band

6    and despite feeling superior to him

| | |
|---|---|
| 0 | you sunk to his murderous level, murdering now |
| | what I consider precious, challenging my |
| | outflanking opinion as put forward in the Great |
| | Chain of Being, reversing |
| 8 | Foucault's philosophical treatise on modern corporeal |
| | punishment as |
| 4 | a demonstration of power. |
| 1 | I |
| 2 | am ashamed |
| 8 | to say that I haven't philosophically prepared you |
| 4 | for an only child's |
| 8 | compelling sense of worth, for a lack of |
| 8 | nakedness, for much less free time, my crimson |
| 6 | gorilla mask pressed against your belly's |
| 2 | velvet doughnut. |
| 6 | I am also ashamed to say |
| 9 | I have eaten all your offerings without sharing even |
| 4 | a morsel of that |
| 5 | perfectly auspicious mango that you |
| 6 | served with creamy, grated young coconuts |
| 0 | that you were perhaps saving for a succulent |
| | eventide. Give up |
| 4 | your neurotic therapy session |
| 2 | with the |
| 4 | devil, who is still |
| 1 | charging |
| 9 | an outrageous price per session. Her hourly rate is |
| 6 | between a duodecillion and a googolplex |
| 5 | for sinners or docile converters |
| 2 | converting the |
| 8 | bitcoin of cardinal sins to the ethereum of |
| 5 | sensual mango desserts. It's that |

0   lack of preeminent encouragement from my fallen
son—
2   farmer, foiled
2   mendicant, divine
2   spawn, spurned.
1   You
0   have yet to illuminate your profane motive
6   to mediocrely mirror my ex-wife, Lucifer's,
6   outlook on 'brotherly love' and fashion.
1   I
1   can't
8   emphasize how divinely uncomfortable I am about
your
6   UGG stilettos and haberdasher's waxy moustache.
3   I expect you
0   to manifest your gender expression more tactfully, or
at least less loudly.
6   Homophobia isn't my primary native language
7   but you know that I am fluent
4   in bestowing grief unnecessarily
4   so as to teach
2   my subordinates
7   elaborate lessons they do not need to
8   abide by, only to provoke a sanguinary appetite
6   which now you may blame me
2   exhaustively and
2   galactically for.
0   This is to say that, unlike China, I did want a pseudo
granddaughter born from Eve
3   so that she
9   could control the entire, divine half-asset of my
graminaceous

1    fairgrounds.

9    Before Eve conceived you, she drank contaminated
         water from

4    the Citarum River and

9    its fluvial content is filled with estrogen debris and

4    plastic orbs of vitriol.

5    Your insatiable desire for kitchen

0    appliances has de-hammocked my fabled and terrific

4    philosophical and empirical masculinity

7    and has left it fragile as the

1    verglas.

2    I won't

3    pollute your sincerest

7    nose hairs with the perfumed reasons behind

1    my

3    decision to punish

7    your left cheek for wishing to be

8    toward the ground during lucent afternoons when you

6    only wanted to soften the masculine,

9    land that ancient nonsense flat on its back! For

6    it's only a matter of time

0    until I can grieve my political enemy amply.

9    I've always believed, despite my
         supercalifragilisticexpialidocious, omnipotent,
         autarchic power

5    that you might powerfully swim

6    through a time machine and offer

3    me a flowerless

6    wind that travels through the lower

4    regions of your failed

3    mammographic exam while

7    Hart Crane winds eglantine through a videotape.

1   I

9   imagine you confuse my route as someone gravity-
bound and

1   it

7   doesn't help that it traces a through-line

2   into the

8   repressed libidinal parameters that I set for you.

7   I know death is close to you.

4   Here's to the minuscule

6   monkish sexual gaze on your post-trans

7   hallucinations of my obsequious impulses to forgive

7   you. Your scornful sperm de-acquisitions have not

6   unswum the goodness of my mood.

4   Caina, you are the

6   bain I never expected to have.

5   If I have been cruel,

7   as cruel as a renovicting starling, then

5   it's because I love you

7   without any conditions, by which I mean

3   I love you

9   the way a shepherd loves sheep and also mutton.

6   I love you like the way

2   a voracious

4   mute loves head-splitting sound

1   or

3   an hourglass sips

8   sand in both directions, which is to say

9   I love you singularly and only particularly to you.

0   It would be not only impossible as purple lady
slippers blooming in Hades but

8   necessary for the way equity and gender travel

6   (too horizontally for my hierarchical taste)

5     to prefer to love you

8     the way a pirate loves his extirpated leg

3     (with purple lavender

2     lotion slathered

6     over it, with pomegranate seeds pre-soaked

4     in its evening bath).

5     I prefer to love you

9     the way wasps love a globe of curly hair

9     the way an ounce of honey loves a spoon

5     the way a spoon loves

8     the pantyhose of a knife in quotidian time.

1     Were

3     sagebrush and twisted

3     garlic strands lent

9     an anatomical piquant, rapier-like bulbs to the
nightshade family

0     could be named aubergine and atropa belladonna.

4     If named they could

7     fill sometimes with atropine, scopolamine, and
hyoscyamine

8     and if poison and sadness could take great

0     comfort in their mutual ability to bloom and sedate

2     the psychoactive

7     capillary behind your left thigh I'd send

5     divine mixed messages regarding the

9     nature of subtext and its potential for seismological
sunsets.

0     It's so unnatural for you, Caina, to force your brother
to exist outside of time by killing him. Have you
considered

0     what it must be like to slip into a fault plane, to enter
the hypocentre of

9 the graviola, whose soursop's tropical pulse cannot
     tolerate the
9 comparison to dragon skin frequently made by
     various passing
4 monks laced in saffron?
6 Their invented stories are whispered to
5 rice crumbs scattered along the
7 stone walkways beside the murmuring rivers that
6 dance bearishly, soar higher than high
4 in illustrious reaches of
0 roasted salt. Ovoid sea
7 flakes scraped from flat mesh beds in
8 fragments are processed in pelletized auras for
     seraphic
9 gesticulations of paint strokes on the ceiling of my
5 vodka flask. I am this
1 inchoate
2 pregnant cat
6 fatly standing by your patio door.
9 I know you feel like I have inadvertently kicked
4 you out of Eden
6 with my declawed paws and my
8 tummy of souls but it is in fact
3 my pre-born kittens
9 who are writing mean, terrible poems about you.
     Darling,
8 retaliation is the only method in which I
3 train the copious
5 Allen Ginsberg wannabes and the
2 Grendel mothers
5 to motorcycle-ride the moral wave
9 made from susurrations of Eden's trees in fervid winds."

5  "Father, you are so ridiculous

7  to think that I, Caina, might sip

o  the waters from the Lethe in hopes that the murder
      of my brother might slip back into sleep and the
      ethical burden

9  of your lack of amnesia might unboulder itself from

8  the Berlin Wall, the Great Wall of China

2  and Croatia's

5  Walls of Ston. I suffer

8  like a flock of pigeons lifting off at

2  Ben Gurion

2  over canonized

6  airport runways worthy of divine intervention.

2  I exile.

o  Father, love me for my weakness, for my foalish,
      mule-like

5  shoe selections, which render me

2  completely dependent

2  upon a

4  pillowfort rattan wall shelf

8  as a device to lean my body against.

9  Despite being the older sister, I'm small and
      inexperienced,

4  just a lordly minnow.

o  My fallacy has made me lonely, overconfident, and
      although hubris has visited me during the long
      nights in which I fantasized about my brother's
      murder and death, I

7  am still childing within your tantrumic world.

7  I am still a riddle in the

2  skeleton lock

6  fused like a discount crystal pendulum

7    over a tiny recessed eye as if

1    volition

9    were a blinking thing, as if my will was

4    disappointed by the stagecoach

7    shuttling across your vision. My particular piglet

8    soul attempts a swine-like, meat-free redemption. I am

2    not your

6    easy daughter dressed as a biblical

8    guinea pig dipped head to toe in glory.

4    Father, don't you wish

8    you too were closer to the earth, nestling

2    in experience

6    like a french fry under gravy?

0    I dream about you and me, Father—our wild hair
        bunched up in ponytails

1    like

4    we are the wild

7    prairies of Saskatchewan quietly sifting the air

6    on that bootylicious Tesla motorbike you

9    stole from Mars after pretending it was actually yours.

9    I dream of wearing a wool two-piece cochineal bikini.

0    I feed you salmon off a malachite platter wearing
        KISS gel fantasy jelly nails from Wal-Mart

9    and you recite the in-progress ten commandments
        back to

0    yourself between chews, with barely any
        modifications, despite

2    commandment seven

6    having first been about 'adulterating,' not

4    premeditatedly hatching from my

0    extravagant forays into fantasy where

1    sin

3    just means target

6    missed by 2.3 centimetres. I admit

3    this is generous

9    considering that my parents aren't the best role models

4    when it comes to

4    pruning apple trees with

3    bedazzled fake nails

7    while wearing black zipper stilettos highly celebrated

4    by Michelle Obama's secretary.

5    I don't know why I

5    look to you for advice

3    I've always suspected

0    aligned itself with Cold War ideology.

5    You rejected my divine vision

0    of your every descendent donning a hat made of
     jellyfish and thistles.

6    Murder is one thing, but that

8    outright refusal of my jiggling Elysian utopic
     aspiration

2    is just

0    as deadly to the moxie of a burgeoning fashionista

3    as Phoebe Philo's

4    fuchsia crocs with charms.

9    Father, is it possible still for bandage peep toe

6    shoes to banish the folkloric peeping

2    Tom from

5    the peephole of our planet?

2    Is it

4    enough to anoint your

5    myopic tongue as the primary

1    megaphone

7    for the saliva's slick rebirth of itself

4    as conductor of noise?

9    This is to say that I am not sorry

3    for the murderee's

9    last request to sleep on 456 gluten-free blueberry
        pancakes

9    and to sink within a wheat-free dream like syrup.

6    I know you have a high

5    tolerance for 100 percent sugar.

1    I

4    cannot stomach your saccharine

3    imagination, which has

1    tussled

4    my destructive relationship with

2    rhinestones and

9    Abel's highly chlorinated swimming pool, which ebbs
        and flows

8    according to the fourteen known moons of Neptune.

0    Father, I have regretted decapitating Abel. You have
        already spent your Gregorian calendar days
        persuading me so, but

9    it was an inevitable act for the 'common good'

1    to

9    protect your multitudinous unimpeachable buxom
        flocks of fat-tailed sheep

0    and to protect your relentless, potentially specious,
        potentially naive philosophy that even murder is a
        good (and even necessary) thing for the universe's
        quantum metaphysical motto:

6    'For the bible tells me so.'

5    You and I are not

9    exactly twins but sisters like my eyebrows or your

2    fallopian monuments

5    named by an Italian anatomist

0    which is to say that you and I are not gatekeepers of
        morality and despite bestowing my biological, that
        is to say unholy, father the lexical rights to name
        things in this material world, you

9    decide to 'leave it at that' like an unfinished

3    Tour de France

7    while I hurl my bike into lavender.

2    I'm sorry

2    dear bicycle

1    I

6    wasn't thinking of your metaphorical well-being.

9    I was thinking about impaling yellow bell peppers on

6    each peg of your golden crown.

4    I was thinking about

6    the spiciness of my organic carrots

1    and

5    the buxomness of my blueberries

1    and

5    the pom-poms of my lettuces!

7    I know, in my carelessness, I've deflated

0    your kiddie pool into a flat dab stifling a circular
        patch of grass on your holy lawn while you were in it.

9    I know anything metaphysical is a young Napoleon
        waiting

8    for a horse he can mount while wearing

5    XL chainmail designed by 16th-century

8    secretive oath-based unemployed metal workers who
        hated to

3    disregard mediaeval sexiness

8    despite the proliferation in habits and 'hell's capes'

7    and despite the conquistador's bullets passing through

4    poorly sized peep holes.

1    I

0    still want to support local businesses and sexiness in
        general, which

5    is my way of rebelling.

9    So you see, Father, our motivations and desires are

7    not isolated concubines tucked away like Rapunzel's

8    basketball shorts, which have never made it into

8    the NBA like you had so badly wanted.

5    You loved her, despite her

9    small, petite fetish for Kobe Bryant's post-death
        heliotropic debris

5    which had certainly disturbed thee.

9    Rapunzel, a hysterical vixen before a suicidal brick
        well!

7    So you conceded to her interest in

7    a pre-existing product fashioned for her harangued

2    split ends.

9    So you see, Father, when I retaliated against your

7    gendered haircuts or hair-growings, I wanted to

5    demonstrate that my body isn't

4    capable of fostering excessive

9    carpathian bell-flowers sunk knee-deep in a
        hilariously mediaeval pot.

8    I need roots, in fact, deep in soil.

9    Father, have you forgotten to water me in the

3    light of your

0    excessive love for my brother?

1    I

6    hold you accountable for Abel's death

1    because

7    if you had loved us both equally

| | |
|---|---|
| 5 | I would not have been |
| 3 | profoundly motivated to |
| 9 | redisperse your love through annihilation, which may have been |
| 2 | the proper |
| 8 | way of going about it since your love |
| 4 | still in its infant |
| 6 | stage, hadn't yet reached full unconditionality. |
| 8 | We both are unwilling students of murder, you |
| 1 | see. |
| 3 | The bloodbath of |
| 8 | my regret spills into my ability to sleep. |
| 2 | And you |
| 6 | sleep like a baby even though |
| 8 | the war of conscience should have been a |
| 6 | shared event because you invented me! |
| 8 | I am just a demigod, a small mirror |
| 3 | of your garden. |
| 8 | Sitting on the upper echelon of moral ideals |
| 6 | is an uncute look for you. |
| 8 | How shall I punish you, Father? Your lack |
| 9 | of restorative justice unconitionally upsets me. Law and order |
| 4 | are not bathroom jokes |
| 2 | but rather |
| 7 | pregnant tortoises waddling in your sea-blue water |
| 7 | unable to turn either left or right. |
| 4 | I would punish you |
| 1 | but |
| 5 | you've a way of depleting |
| 5 | my desire to camp within |
| 9 | the bureau of consular affairs where the state department |

9  has become obsessed with the euphemistic
       etymology of 'overseas'
1  and
8  would like to remove the s and revert
5  'COVID-19' to 'Mandatory Mandarin Oranges'
5  the kind wrapped in papers
9  pressed between the flotsam of saliva and Egyptian
       papyrus
2  which is
5  where you originated the idea
2  for Oreos
4  and the Great Flood
5  an odd but powerful combination.
9  I might distinguish the limited but protean range of
5  the ever-increasing spectrum of grizzledness.
3  My delirium has
9  eyes that are nothing like the moons within Oreos
5  which Mordecai, before he auspicated,
9  pointed out while twisting off the top cookie layer.
4  With your slow appetite
3  you turn to
1  the
0  next chapter of the poem, and bid my herbaceous
       MTV cribs episode adieu, peppering my fraught
       botanical escapades and unholy schisms with
       post-murder pillowtalk.
4  Like a nun, you
9  turn to Mordecai in the secret polyester sweat of
9  Jewish damnation, whose exilic pontifications have
   set sail haphazardly
7  into the ears of an exiled queen."

2   "I, Mordecai,

5   do intend to find mini

2   motor oil

4   spills on your vast

6   erections as a disorganized sign of

8   your un(re)productive but fervent penchant for ill-
     advised mechanophilia.

o   I am no omnipotent figure and certainly I am no
     supervillain Mr. Freeze, but may I remind you that
     if you weren't busy having sex with IBM and 3D
     house printing machines, you would have been
     able to stop Cain or Caina (is it?) from murdering
     Abel

8   which, in my opinion, is a useful direction

4   toward reverse and inverse

5   time-bending. This is to say

9   that you are allowed to make anachronistic mistakes,
     God

8   but this one, the obscene 3D print-out included,

7   is not for the wayward retail propaganda

2   of your

7   decision to hide the red beryl from

3   your final will.

6   Time is quite inconsiderate. At times

4   engendering belief in regularity.

4   But a stone is

6   a decoration of the heart, not

9   gaudy wallpaper for diluting your damaged
     relationship with remorse.

5   The way you neglected Abel's

8   unmorbid, nostalgic request to keep the fratricidal
       stone
4   ornamenting the garden pond
8   is a moralistic gesture that envy is no
6   vice for which he must absolve
5   himself in the short time-
3   frame of premeditation.
8   The Persian Empire was too intensely busy housing
3   Jewish exiles and
6   young virgins who abhorred olive oil
7   atop their nests of spaghetti, opting for
3   hazelnuts drizzled in
6   the tears of a hundred turduckens
2   bird saliva
2   baked alaska
2   broccoli flakes
6   and vegan galantine suspended in agar-agar.
2   The heart
6   desquamates into a consommé of thoughts.
0   So when I refused to prostrate before that
       milquetoast Haman
9   they decided not only that I kick the bucket
9   but also that I bury my future in coagulated
1   Agag-begat
2   frontal lobe.
4   I am every Jewish
6   first born's forehead that has not
0   been marked to receive God's (questionable) sense of
       justice, nor especially Haman's. My ideological
       soup has been seasoned with brutality and sky-
       high gallows, treacherous thorn-trees and stars in
       the shape of a fish!

8 When I approached Queen Esther to discuss Haman's

0 disdain for my sackcloth, I couldn't understand why
     he would think any other garb would be
     appropriate as a voguish response to his decree

5 that all creatures with knees

1 should

2 buy MOBA—

4 a ploy for distraction.

3 Queen Esther wasn't

8 exactly stoked to be a child bride who

8 sabotaged her feministic, Rabelaisian ideals by
     decoupling the

4 carnival from the carnivalesque

3 assassination devised by

9 Haman to kill her people and me, her uncle

0 because he believed that his ego isn't that fragile.
     Anti-semitic sentiments pursued his soul

4 sisters so why not

5 casually take genocide to the

1 illogical

2 brink of

4 his unbecoming bloodthirsty insanity?

4 Haman, you are my

1 least

3 favourite Ken doll.

6 Your rubber knees don't even bend

5 at a forty-five degree angle

4 which is ironic because

9 neither assassination nor prostration is a hypotenuse.
     The body

7 does not slant upwards toward counterfeit holiness.

6 Haman is the boytoy I imagine

2    who licks

7    his thumb before executing an important political

8    campaign plan spanning the southern United States, mostly

0    along the Bible belts

7    in search of the elusive Bible buckle.

9    Queen Esther commissioned a belt buckle privately with a

7    plumed fan in hand wafting her ambivalence.

7    She wanted a sexually morbid inscription that

1    read

5    astra inclinant, sed non obligant

6    so as to untether Haman from

9    his psychological warfare with karma whose law governs the

1    comings

4    and goings of war-bred

3    ponies with hair-dos

5    shaped like Medusa's triquetra tongue.

9    I pile on top of my life another scoop

9    of pulverized pistachio ice cream and the bleating of

7    Haman. The official had a penchant for

7    lemniscated women in dominant positions, terrifying heights

0    and lemon-scented petitions signed by oil-abhorring young virgins with extreme dietary preferences.

0    While strolling back and forth in the northern Tower, with his murderous hands behind his back, Haman

1    sneezed

2    out two

9    directives for his henchmen who, unable to understand, dallied

6 with the dyadic Samson-like flamboyant gladiators

1 instead.

6 Not too highly skilled in the

0 area of pro wrestling, Haman decided to scale the
political ranks and eschew his athletic theatrical
exhibitionism, allowing his enemies

8 within the insouciant Persian supremacy to blithely
discredit

9 the legitimacy of his wearing a topless wrestling toga.

4 Nipple exposure has given

4 Haman a false sense

1 of

6 third-wave feminism and Esther cannot handle

9 masculine men whose man-nipples have some
discoloration or whose

4 costumes betray wrestling failures

8 of biblical proportions. Proportions seen on a
Calvinist

6 scale, however, might suggest they happened

8 to be already doomed. A hen coop is

5 designed metaphysically but also predeterminedly

5 for it houses both chickens

5 and eggs and therefore certainly

8 damnation. Haman reasoned that breast de-
augmentation requires nipple

4 castings just in case

8 the breast is like a kitchen pot, its

4 mammaplasty botchable. He imagined

0 its lids could be removed for pre-steaming closure

6 and fitted back again nicely, so

3 as to hide

5 their marshmallowy exuberant bubbling contents—

| | |
|---|---|
| 3 | contents Haman furtively |
| 4 | associates with Caina, despite |
| 2 | how irrationally |
| 2 | his fantasy |
| 0 | has wrinkled its culinary nose like his uncle's. Ophidian |
| 7 | appetites for warm and little beings with |
| 2 | no waterproof |
| 2 | sleeping bags |
| 2 | will save |
| 5 | biblical rulers from temporary wrath |
| 8 | and save little beings from edible religion. Haman |
| 2 | didn't count |
| 8 | on Queen Esther spiking his soup with campylobacter |
| 4 | spiralling pink into his |
| 8 | soft lentils with some recalcitrant cilantro floating on |
| 8 | its slick surface. Olive oil is an atmosphere |
| 6 | and broth is an afterthought procured |
| 4 | from bone marrow and |
| 8 | from an episode in the life of a |
| 1 | peppercorn. |
| 5 | Its belly, five millimetres in |
| 8 | diameter, does not mean it is not big-hearted. |
| 4 | Cell walls cannot reform |
| 5 | one's criminal instincts or biological |
| 6 | genetic drifts. Haman reasoned that time |
| 0 | is not on his side so long as I, Mordecai, am farming the chickens for his soup and commissioning his adopted daughter to cook a 'wrestler's portion' of toxicological chicken noodle |
| 2 | to appease |
| 8 | her distaste at his scheme to eradicate her. |
| 5 | She doesn't take it personally |

0    though she understands carrying a heavy load will
     eventually make a person feel lighter. Thus, she
     accepts her chef-like vocation at the behest of her
     avuncular father figure.
6    After all, genocide isn't just wallpaper
0    you choose in your childhood in the hue of Pepto-
     Bismol.
1    It
6    isn't just a box you flatten
8    nor an ideological door you sand down quickly
4    nor a vintage knob.
2    Wholesale slaughter
7    is not easily mixed into a bowl
3    with cilantro and
9    spring onions and heirloom tomatoes chopped into
     pristine cubes.
4    History tells us that
5    genocide is so painfully ordinary.
2    Not worthy
2    of eradication.
6    When Russia sent skillful farmers to
7    farm the cool crisp plains of snow
4    astronomical famine followed. The
6    lonely plow horse of idiotic decrees
7    shuffles again to the gulag's nival edge
6    and grows colossal in the eye
7    of North Korea. To deal with one's
8    gulag of the soul by kidnapping movie stars
8    and stealing their wealth, submerging their fame
     beneath
9    an ocean of radio waves doesn't invisibilize their
     sorrow.

| | |
|---|---|
| 5 | The films they produced exhibited |
| 2 | no real |
| 5 | conjugal identity. With macabre vectors |
| 2 | of directionlessness |
| 1 | actors |
| 3 | favour parties. They |
| 8 | bind and recombine for imperial impact. Being forced |
| 5 | to eat off Esther's spoon |
| 2 | was something |
| 2 | like impregnating |
| 5 | a queer doorbell with the |
| 4 | ability to pour lava |
| 9 | into choral ambient sound. Mimicking slowly China's revolutionary opera |
| 9 | coloraturas and soubrettes, Haman filled his coquettish tessituras with |
| 5 | counterrevolutionary ideals such as pointing |
| 4 | one's finger toward Lucifer's |
| 6 | curly chest hair by Hieronymus Bosch. |
| 6 | Guido Reni's rippling panoramic beefcake trapezoids |
| 6 | marries Ryuichi Sakamoto's Thousand Knives in |
| 7 | a wild jalopy ride to peyote's end. |
| 2 | Haman's rural |
| 7 | preference for captured chicken and wrangled pig |
| 8 | begat a poorly executed and poorly planned liquidation |
| 2 | of recipes. |
| 3 | Queen Esther's servants |
| 9 | much preferred Lucifer's burnt toast to Esther's nefarious stews. |
| 8 | They also preferred Nehemiah's cured rabbits over Jeremiah's |

6    penchant for sea snails slurped raw.

4    The Second Temple war

5    was what Haman had predicted

6    situated at the heart of history's

5    sloshing lychee fruit double martini.

9    The bartender, the Persistent Widow, often stared at the

6    shape of refusal as a way

1    into

1    God's

6    extraterrestrial footnotes. Her impersonal edits on

3    the role of

5    exculpation after a sinner's Alzheimer's

4    diagnosis, the widow redacted

8    for the sake of transforming God's Reuleaux triangle

8    into a more precise throwing star. She could

6    triangulate God's tripolar manic-depressive holy ghost

2    into equi-sized

3    curvilinear jelly beans

0    flavoured after rhymes, such as pear-éclair, plum-rum,
       and pineapple-snapple

5    to rid the religion of

7    bland orthomolecular secularism. Not in this picture

7    am I eating plum-rum jelly beans by

4    candlelight muttering to myself:

5    'King Ahasuerus is so boring.

6    He is as boring as snow-flavoured

4    mud.' I then set

9    aside my thoughts of mediocrity and set to clean

8    my soul so I'd not be ill-prepared to

0    get into gardening my sexually blossoming lily pads.
       Haman saw lust at the end of every arm of his
       tentacling thoughts, but I wanted to

3    reduce pussy eating

5    among the dietarily-fussy virgins and

5    sylphs who won't shave their

9    armpits nor obey the dresscode of no bifurcated
        nether-garments.

3    It's so clear

6    that Haman does not have my

3    virgins pre-selected for

4    ousting like he has

5    with his. He prefers his

6    coffee with a pot of honey

8    and his women unfiltered and filthy as in

1    splattered

7    with onomanic debris from the Gobi Desert.

4    Their chocolate cookie crumbs

3    hang from the

2    lowest rafter.

4    My ache to exist

1    never

1    mingles

2    with octogenarians.

5    It's rare to wake up

1    singing.

5    In dialogues that have the

0    emotional beefiness of arias, I flex the sound of

7    flowers being whiplashed by Jeff Bezos's space

6    link eeling across my corrugated vision.

0    Time has been berated softly by Cardano's Ouroboros
        and Haskell's language of

6    pure functionality and saucy nineteenth-century idioms.

9    Haman, deeply influenced by Haskell's laziness and
        long back

4    ladled himself a bowl
7    of itchy pythons, cucumber draped in Polynesian
9    manta ray tattoos and edible succulents made into salsa.
4    While waiting for Ahasuerus
5    to wander the desert in
1    overalls
0    and so shatter in a rather asinine fashion his
         reputation against the melting sunset, Haman
9    bared the raisin of his soul in a way
6    that made Esther fall in love
5    with yellow bell peppers grown
9    by Haman's neighbours beside land yachts in the
         mountains.
6    These bell peppers looked so radiant
0    they made Esther want to sleep naked, and run off
         chirping into a rainstorm, or swallow a meadowful
         of sunlight.
9    To run as fast as she could to the
4    forehead of approaching dawn
0    so that her legs could kiss
2    the city
5    and its cloistered, manic siblings
2    hovering nearby.
2    Esther wasn't
8    necessarily wanting to be free, just a ripple
8    swirling in the clairvoyant beam of an estuary.
7    Like the moment you are born, without
9    a pack of e-cigarettes attached to your umbilical cord
7    but wanting them, so full of want
1    so
0    full
8    of loss, so full of unprotected agony, so

9 full of desire that one's platonic herb garden grow
3 so massively fast
1 that
4 the corridors to light
5 extend to even the roots
6 beyond the chthonic material of turnips
6 and into the articulation of worm-trails!
9 If Esther had wanted to end her herbal addiction
1 well
3 it was impossible.
6 Since herbs were invented to produce
8 unexpected remedies at unexpected intervals in the body's
6 forensic insatiable drifts they breed envy
7 and resurrect new, expensive bacchanalian pagan
　 churches."

2 Esther said,
2 "To surrender
8 would be to already have known evening. When
7 the cypress trees with their long legs
4 made of shadows dangle
8 on the Mississippi marsh floor like some tenebrous
9 hairs sunk to the bottom of a tub, always
4 eye your political schemes
0 through tangles and through sludge. I wouldn't
5 conceive of bringing your men
6 to renovate my heart's shabby preferences.
0 Nor, I say, to mouthpiece their monotheistic
1 revisions
0 as a possible hypothetical deconstruction of God's
　 ephemeral plan to negate India's
1 hundred

5     thousand COVID cases. Your speech,
0     sweet uncle, has led to overwhelming questions that
          when posed spurred
3     insurmountable grief. Infernos
3     rub up against
0     the gay man babysitting a corpse, his lover of three
          years, out in the open air, for eighteen hours,
          waiting for it to be cremated, and
8     if this gesture is not a question then
6     it is a reference toward God's
1     etherizing
7     me. I am no child of the
9     Shakespearean canon that might have me asking
          'wherefore' or
2     is Hamlet
8     really dead or is he just out wayfaring
6     with other deceased Princes of Denmark
8     or off on a mission like Rosencrantz and
0     Guildenstern. Theatrical figures pretend to coexist
          with the
9     mind's exquisite laquearia damaged with cigarette
          smoke and perfume.
2     Your coalesced
0     stories, uncle, may continue but will continue
          together like eggs and toast mixed on a plate
8     of pre-bathed rose wreaths and Danish golden stars
7     salvaged from garage sales in coastal cities.
4     Flooded by the loquacious
7     chatter of the sea coming and leaving
6     I feel so massively old and
0     yet have the hunger of something new. Such are
          time's masquerades.

| 9 | My ornery heart renews labyrinths of aging despair yet |
| 1 | distracts |
| 7 | me from bearing the plausible fruits of |
| 8 | my laborious efforts to reconsider what passion is. |
| 2 | Afterall, I |
| 4 | angle my soul toward |
| 9 | the impossible, which is where the nephew of passion |
| 3 | disdains his father |
| 8 | and succumbs to his young mother's impulsive |
|   | tendencies |
| 5 | to take signs for wonders |
| 8 | and all aftermaths for ridicules. I know I |
| 9 | have lingered too long in the chambers of the |
| 0 | famished. I know if I keep on eating and eating and |
|   | eating my raw, ill-prepared emotions away, I could |
|   | find |
| 0 | the stone amid all the weeping lushness dripping |
|   | down my chin. |
| 9 | I could teach raw honey how to be mermaidish. |
| 7 | And I could teach my human voice |
| 1 | to |
| 4 | meticulously swell, full of |
| 9 | raspy vibrations, sonic exuberance from my youthful, |
|   | clairvoyant days. |
| 0 | Once I was chimes in a hurricane and felt that fear |
|   | could never |
| 9 | release its tombstone of misgiving, bury me. Of my |
| 6 | obliterating vertical horizon, I fall into |
| 7 | it with this archaic disbelief that my |
| 5 | heart belongs to the mantle |
| 9 | when in reality, the suppression of a winter phoenix |
| 8 | is only as effective as a ball under |

| | |
|---|---|
| 5 | a birch canoe drifting unconsciously |
| 2 | as ache. |
| 6 | You surface your transfixed blade for |
| 1 | incision. |
| 3 | I suppose it |
| 6 | wouldn't hurt to illuminate the undergrowth |
| 5 | of moths inside a Lasko |
| 5 | wind curve tower fan to |
| 4 | articulate the inevitable philosophy |
| 9 | that one must find a bigger wing to be |
| 7 | at peace with the fourth dimension of |
| 8 | living. Yes, time is anything but a line |
| 1 | in |
| 8 | the surface of a bog made with your |
| 9 | transient, negligent request for a gender-friendly redistribution of labour. |
| 3 | I finish my |
| 1 | trivial |
| 2 | spoonful of |
| 9 | Lebanese garlic sauce—concocted quickly by the new cook |
| 7 | Ahasuerus picked off like a goldfish from |
| 8 | the Temple of Jerusalem. Toum isn't made for |
| 4 | just anybody, it requires |
| 8 | a high tolerance for allinase and Zgharta and |
| 2 | the feeling |
| 1 | of |
| 6 | being in love with a potato. |
| 8 | It is true that unnecessary things shouldn't be |
| 2 | underestimated or |
| 9 | taken to the edge of the French Polynesian abyss |
| 9 | and tossed in like any other type of love. |

8    I am a bed of lettuce and you

9    are the darkling beetle in its heart. I wanted

4    sliced Brandywine tomato as

8    if it were an organ that bled salt

7    and seaweed and Volcanic Hill Cabernet Sauvignon

2    and doldrums

2    and dacquoise

6    and every possible answer to the

5    nature of sparkling water. When

8    it decided to spontaneously explode even when left

8    in the imminent care of a subservient geological

0    force that was meant to quell the spontaneity of water
       and turbulent air and calms and squalls and light
       baffling winds

4    I told you all

8    my secrets. Nevertheless, you never climb the outer

5    rim of Saturn for my

7    mindful derivations of your cruellest ideations, which

5    leads me to forbid you

6    to eat the soup I so

4    dispassionately and apathetically contaminate

0    with uncooked stinging nettle sprinkled on top as if a
       delicate herbal garnish from my abundant
       vegetable garden.

1    It

4    is so satisfying to

2    nonchalantly extirpate

7    the soft walls of your mandible by

0    making things irresistibly impossible and then
       possible again. For

4    example, food and other

7    orally affiliated activities such as a blowjob

| | |
|---|---|
| 7 | or just a popsicle, though it might |
| 5 | glaucously, sarcolinely, mikadoishly, coquelicotilly, fulvously, |
| 5 | unboldenly, detribously, mismettlingly, disleagueredly, remetricatedly |
| 5 | untimely, deliberately, misanthropically, displeasingly, repetitiously |
| 1 | bedraggle |
| 3 | your c-level morals. |
| 2 | Oh, whimsical |
| 3 | sadness for advanced |
| 7 | levels of Buddhism attainable only by gleaning |
| 9 | with the lazy owls whose eyes continue to widen |
| 6 | even in the darkest parts of |
| 4 | the painting's umber granular |
| 1 | chipping! |
| 4 | After the Philistines assaulted |
| 5 | the garden soil with old |
| 1 | coffee |
| 5 | I wept beneath the grove |
| 2 | and imagined |
| 3 | three acorn hats |
| 7 | having a poised, semi-philosophical discourse on the |
| 4 | nature of beret-wearing seeds. |
| 6 | The ones who struggle with pollinated |
| 2 | plants have |
| 3 | hirsute dreams about |
| 4 | Boris Pasternak and his |
| 3 | inexorable lung cancer |
| 6 | prompting him to reflect on the |
| 4 | nature of human suffering |
| 5 | in the form of poetry. |

4   I completely relate to
2   the line
8   'Man is born to live, not to prepare
5   meals endlessly for ungrateful kings
8   who ever still cling to their mother's teats
4   as if cliff edges
4   were elongated and milky
4   and caused utter fascination.'
7   For Nate Silver who created a spreadsheet
9   that despite failing to predict Donald Trump's gloomy
     erection
5   was able to augur the
2   predicament I
6   so untimely fashioned in mathematical anticipation
5   that 'the future is female.'
8   Afterall, when Joanna Russ wrote *The Female Man*
6   and invented the utopia of Whileaway
7   my period shifted into erratic traffic light
8   signals, a ceaseless flashing red confusing every passage
2   of my
1   muscular
0   masculinity, which has remained dormant and
     Jewish and female until I began having
     intermittent nocturnal
5   visions of my neighbour's cat.
1   Scratching
1   oblivion
4   into a lamp, I
1   mewl
3   petroleum and pesticide
5   riddles turned into the crepuscular
4   embankment of my posture

7  against my bedpost when I'm feeling imminently
3  insecure about the
5  status of my relationship. On
7  edge, Ahasuerus moves through an insectile abyss
3  iridescently as a
9  clumsy bricklayer taking a forbidden nap near the
      arches
5  of his collapsible unfinished work.
2  I reason
3  we are not
1  that
1  embittered
3  with insolent feelings
4  teetering on the precipice
2  while contemplating
7  the nature of dragonflies exiting their nymphs.
1  Without
6  feeling at least a little bit
6  famished or enraged, I also reason
1  that
0  life is too short and vacuous and not paratactical enough
2  or peripatetic
1  enough
3  to be able
5  to climb the terrace of
9  our potential polyamorous arrangement. He peers
      down at my
6  slick titanium-made chariot, still so silvery
9  even after years of driving to and from his
5  synapomorphic sorghum storage space after
3  swilling our mouths
6  with 2018 Cab Sau found deep

2    in Mordecai's

3    dormant wine cellar.

1    I

4    took four quick sips

4    before I manhandled the

2    lemonade pitcher

9    and tossed it asunder so that it radically shattered

5    against the insolent chariot like

2    deadly fireworks.

4    There is something impossible

8    in the shape of an ignited bloom falling.

4    There is something impossible

9    to uncover under the surface of Ahasuerus's look after

3    I turn the

7    poem he wrote at the edge of

1    the

8    patch of Bishop's Crown Mordecai planted months ago

7    into song. I hesitate to name emotions

1    that

1    appear

0    to require metaphor and the scaffolding of language
          including adverbs and adjectives for fear that I
          might fill them weakly like rain in a tire, on its
          side, with a hole in it, in the yard I grew up in.

1    I

4    cannot stoop to write

5    while God negates the femininity

7    of my Internet connection. All the while

6    I struggle to have the proper

5    bandwidth for my multiple cybernetic

4    antics with their antlers

0    poised at the cardinal call of my machine gun heart."

## Love Song Between Light and Darkness

3 It goes without

5 saying that the heart's bullets

9 can hit targets as far away as 20,000 metres

0 over and over—yes, they can snipe yours in perfect
    bright red bull's-eyes

2 without binoculars.

7 So when you run across the border

9 with a boxful of endangered livestock buried in the

9 Alaskan birthday pie I made for you, be careful.

3 I am led

4 to believe that you

4 are rarely ready to

0 own up to your egregious, erroneous modes of
    making decisions pertaining to the well-being of

3 my damaged left

7 ventricle rabbiting erratically through each long-lived
    moodswing.

4 My love and yours

2 ne'er fester

0 unlike Noah's mind when God promoted him to be
    the CEO of

0 Animal Rights, involving incisive and cruel decisions
    expelling dinosaurs and unicorns

7 from the ark. Architecturally speaking, what was

3 a practical choice

1 turned

0 criminal after the enormous skeletons were
    exhumed, after the unicorn horns were found and
    made into ornate necklaces dangling around the
    sweaty necks of conquerors.

5 Noah has always been my

7 fitspiration, but in this regard I feel

8 somewhat deterred by his long legs and his

5 lack of last-minute architectural ingenuity.

3 Na'amah, Noah's brilliant

9 demonic cutie pie who makes babies from dreaming of

0 "miracle whip" and "delight," had advised Noah
    repeatedly that he ought to create a quantum space
    or a quantum moment for the existence (and
    escort) of the dyadic Argentinian Dreadnoughtus
    schrani into the ark, a place where space could be
    folded over and over again. She said, he must
    think of space as an origami and the dreadful
    Dreadnoughtuses

6 as a twin tower on its

2 colossal girth

1 sideways.

9 Afterall, I've always viewed the Dreadnoughtuses as a
    door

8 to my sauropodal assessment of your lack of

3 authoritative control over

8 decisions requiring the distribution of volume and
    mass

7 of 52 metres and 120 metric tons

4 which is why we're

4 not as biologically diversified

7 and therefore requiring of vestments and vaccines

8 for the unforeseeable but foreseeable you-name-it
    variants circulating

0 like murder hornets into unsuspecting hives. By
    attacking naturopathic honey bees they decapitate
    my once strong will to

| | |
|---|---|
| 8 | blame Noah for painting the Dreadnoughtsuses' toenails in |
| 4 | toxic carnivorous nail polish |
| 7 | the colour of 2018 Mountains Proprietary Red |
| 8 | wine, the wine we drank during our golden |
| 4 | post Late Cretaceous Period |
| 8 | farewell party. You made tipsy speeches about time, |
| 9 | fashion, and those long dreadful hours waiting for the |
| 6 | train to a new bubbling era— |
| 8 | the kind of era that won't extradite Wanzhou. |
| 3 | The congregated rivers |
| 3 | of diplomatic hostage |
| 2 | melt into |
| 1 | coetaneous |
| 4 | impulses bent on destruction. |
| 4 | Unlike a river, Huawei |
| 5 | Technologies' chief financial officer oft-residing |
| 7 | in a "myriad prefecture" isn't entirely drawn |
| 1 | toward |
| 3 | Michael Spavor's unfavourable |
| 8 | luck in his connections, is dressed in pink |
| 6 | the colour of pseudo-espionage. Spavor is |
| 8 | sentenced to many years in prison. In my |
| 7 | Jerusalem, which held my beloved myrrh exporter |
| 5 | captive for three fortnights without |
| 1 | chicken |
| 9 | fingers or tater tots to quell his appetite for |
| 4 | damnation, I heard weeping. |
| 3 | Alas, my beloved |
| 5 | station in life won't allow |
| 0 | me to fulfil my to-do list in one fell swoop and free you, my lover, from your unjust myrrh-initiated |

immurement, which is my third-biggest priority
scrawled in capital letters and taped to my
refrigerator!

6  Let me forcefully remind you that
4  desire should not be
3  sacrificed for the
0  sake of one's well-being, that drinking green juices
   and making soups for my staff and thinking "out
   loud" as you call it is tremendously crucial in light of
2  my mental
1  rabbiting.
8  I used to wake up to news of
4  puppy litters being born
5  into school shootings. Or to
3  sad dads extolling
1  the
9  adolescent benefits of having read *Infinite Jest* instead of
1  sedating
0  their baffling urges to sink themselves in the
   underworld of their extremely detailed diary entries
   during long summers of dread and hatred.
4  Well water lingers in
8  the shooter's mother's backyard. It wasn't she who
4  told COVID to retreat
8  into its wee doom beaker and thus reverse
1  the
0  psychogeographical domination of not just land but
   time, rendering the two as curtain and widow,
   one being slowly pulled across the other.
0  Like most things that engender anxiety separation, is
   it possible still, as I lay awake this morning,
   measuring the Plagues of Egypt against

5    impending ignominious epidemics, to want

3    to convert emotionally

7    into an otter holding hands with another?

0    I want you to see that it is messy, Hitchcock-murder
        messy, to be a biblical chemist without concerns
        for others. After all, the unethical exchanges of
        converting water into blood and later water into
        wine have the possibility of

6    making soldiers believe coconut water can

1    prevent

4    wounds from bleeding when

6    holy water, despite its divine virtues

8    is the actual scam. I have doused myself

0    my brother, you, my earrings and sandals, my
        camels and my water buffalos and the wheat and
        rice fields, and even my

6    ladle in stagnant pools of miracle-water

7    and yet, nothing has healed us from

4    the tyranny of infatuation

9    and from being the diabolical spark that introduced
        genocide

1    into

9    the collective consciousness of the Hitler-like, Stalin-
        like, Mussolini-like, the

2    Dust Bowl–like

7    The Khmer Rouge–like. Like Pol Pot's symbol

8    for dead flowers, or fissures, for paste or

1    for

9    poverty, for sudden clouds or drenched strangers, for
        strong

1    tribunal

1    urges

9   you bring the highly unapologetic kombucha to the
        ampuchea
7   killing machine. Production as a means to
9   start collective farming and end Cambodia's
        relationship with famine
3   deposits beginners' lamentations.
9   With the inability to drink fermented rice wine and
9   harbour a disproportionate fidelity to disobedient
        laws of physics
5   I reason my time here
2   is shortening.
o   The ionized lives of my desire want to be intricate
        and beautiful but still I could fit perfectly into
        someone's long-forgotten memory. I could end
        radical agrarian ideology—and I feel like I have
        by thwarting genocide with my eight-ounce
        champagne-
6   flavoured breasts and my soup recipes.
1   I
4   must hang like a
1   bat
9   to complete the iconography and present my ultimate
        query:
6   Are my breasts exactly like Marie
6   Antoinette's? Or are they more like
3   twin micro-tornados uncorking
4   the prosecco of desire
2   into the
8   mare liberum between Finland and Sweden? Without
        the
7   foggiest notion of sustainable Petrarchan love I
5   pen the following iambic dimeter:

4   The way a door
4   will skim the floor
4   and run the flow
0   of strangers in / and out is like / the way a rose /
       recoils around / a stamen in / my red bouquet.
       The metre collapses. Because each thought of
       you is a stranger passing with a look of hope
       but shaking their head no / no / no / no /
       no—

6   ... Even tomatoes in aluminium cans can
4   in a pinch be
3   too enthusiastic for
7   the poetry of hard living, so I
4   breathe through my nostril
5   the right and the left
1   with
2   utmost concentration.
3   The nightshade family
7   has been my refuge from each little
1   bosom-genocide
8   and yours too, I hope, since I never
1   conceive
9   of you engaging with such enormous and earth-
       shattering problems
2   from the
1   heart
7   with such inconceivable indifference toward my
       need
9   to treasure, shock, lash, slump, clasp, brood, instruct,
       intensify.
9   The Me Too, Trans Rights, anti-Police Brutality, and
       Chipko

9    movements have shepherded, heightened, bolted, launched, magnified, and defaustified

8    their engine of equity with the kind of

3    specialized recipe I

9    had stolen brutishly from the 23rd century A.D. via

1    hacking

0    the quantum mainframe of God's saliva. Its ferocious lubrication during his grand lecture to Adam and Eve in the midst of their expulsion, spat and fired outwardly toward me through time and space, like a Brobdignagian sprinkler or a peacock fanning widely its eye-like feathers

1    and

5    I had no choice but

9    to irrigate your mind's ear with my prolix diatribe.

1    Saliva

9    has electroplated every single hailstone radish I prepared for

5    the critical, epoch-making role you

6    convinced me to galactically and fatally

1    seize.

8    The fluorescence endowed by your citrus-pickled radish recipe

1    softly

4    highlights my cheekbones in

6    the same panjandrumary fashion as the

7    smell of menstrual blood highlights a shark's

5    sudden capricious appetite to open

1    a

4    canister in its jaw

2    with Herculean

6    blindsightedness. I have always been this

9    mix of a modern metropolitan diva and a frustrated

1    ballroom

2    dancing throwback

3    unlike Lady Gaga

9    or Eurydice. My bookmobile of delights endures my taste

7    but my travelling van saturated in fur

4    against cirrus cloud backdrops

8    has decided to roll into the sea overnight

9    and I cannot help but see its passing with

4    an unbearable agony. The

0    swarming of tears across my vision makes me
        wonder, at times, if I'm really blind and not just
        suffering, since I can no longer concentrate on
        objects in sharp relief.

9    I bought that beloved van in an automobile auction

0    which was foretold by God in his speech to Adam and
        Eve.

7    It was to be the van for

1    the

8    Second Coming. The one God designated for Jesus

6    #2, of the "voluptuous mind" according

4    to Lucifer's second mistress

9    who possessed Immanuel Kant, wanting him to "exit
        natural

4    categorical imperatives and ethical

2    public voids"

3    as a means

1    to

9    enact, finally, Corinthians 4:16-18, "So we do not lose

6    heart." Though outwardly we are wasting

1    saliva.

## EPILOGUE

Alas, we have lost heart. Or so it seems after three thousand and two lines of poetry (pi to 3,000 decimal places). But this is merely the first of many (infinite) volumes. To write this book, we foolishly cancelled our memberships with loneliness and wrote across countries, in virtual high seas, daily, for years, spooling out line after line of ancient questions, complaints, pleas, declarations, each taking a line, poets' do-si-do. While we wrote, we got to know each other for the first time. We chatted about our lives, our loves, our families, our pain, our pasts, what we were eating, cooking, planting, not planting, buying, teaching, reading, painting, who was visiting, who was publishing, and whether the heart is really located under the floorboards, as Poe suggested. (It is.) This side chat, perhaps the most precious document of all, maps an epistolary acquaintance, charts a friendship in the making, and *Mechanophilia* is its shadow, its dream, its under-the-floorboards heart, friendship's supraliminality. We think this is why it gets funnier as it moves along. Like books of the Bible, *Mechanophilia* at its current stage comprises four books, each corresponding to a few thousand digits of pi. This project will continue until we die. This is the first book. A genesis in more ways than one.

## SARAH'S ACKNOWLEDGMENTS

Thank you to Vi Khi Nao, who read her poetry over Zoom in front of a microwave and enchanted me and then became my friend. Thank you to our editor, Stuart Ross, whom I love and admire and am thrilled to be working with again.

Thank you always to my perspicacious writing group: Paige Cooper, Jessie Jones, Jessi MacEachern, Will Vallières, Kasia Van Schaik.

Thank you, also, to my friends and family, who heard a lot about this project and read some of it along the way, in particular (but not limited to) André Babyn, Hilary Bergen, Vera Brumwell, Irene Burgoyne, Eva Crocker, Julia de Montigny, Mara Eagle, James Hawes, Blythe Kingcroft, Jamie Macaulay, Jeff Noh, Liam Sarsfield, Gail Scott, Misha Solomon, Shannon Tien, Lise Weil, Bill Weima, Brandon Wint, Elizabeth Wood, my sisters and parents.

## VI'S ACKNOWLEDGEMENTS

I am in debt to the following folks:

Collaborator & editor: Sarah Burgoyne and Stuart Ross

SWHNM members: Lily Hoang, Dao Strom, Hoa Nguyen, Barbara Tran, MyLoan Dinh, Stacey Tran, Sophia Terazawa

Friends & family: Jessica Alexander, Sharon Alexander, Tania Sarfraz, Daisuke Shen, Seth Tourjee, Jay Ponteri, Brandon Hobson, Sun Yung Shin, my brother, Vỹ, my sisters, Uyên and Vân Anh, Mẹ Ngà, Bố Tân

SARAH BURGOYNE is a Canadian experimental poet. Her second collection, *Because the Sun*, was published with Coach House Books in 2021 and was nominated for the A. M. Klein Prize in Poetry. Her first collection, *Saint Twin* (Mansfield: 2016), was a finalist for the A. M. Klein Prize in Poetry, awarded a prize from l'Académie de la vie littéraire, and shortlisted for a ReLit Award for Poetry. Other works have appeared in journals across Canada and the U.S., have been featured in scores by American composer J. P. Merz, and have appeared with or alongside the visual art of Susanna Barlow, Jamie Macaulay, and Joani Tremblay. Visit www.sarahburgoyne.com.

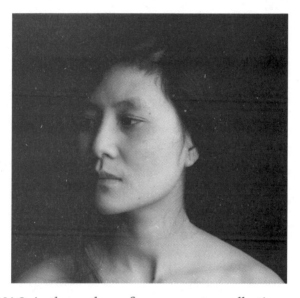

VI KHI NAO is the author of seven poetry collections and of the short-story collection *A Brief Alphabet of Torture* (winner of the 2016 FC2's Ronald Sukenick Innovative Fiction Prize) and the novel *Swimming with Dead Stars*. Her poetry collection *The Old Philosopher* won the Nightboat Books Prize for Poetry in 2014. Her book *Suicide: The Autoimmune Disorder of the Psyche* landed from 11:11 in spring 2023. The fall 2019 fellow at the Black Mountain Institute, she is the author of poetry, fiction, film, and cross-genre collaboration. She was the 2022 recipient of the Jim Duggins Outstanding Mid-Career Novelist Prize.

## Other Feed Dog Books from Anvil Press

"A Feed Dog Book" is an imprint of Anvil Press edited by Stuart Ross and dedicated to contemporary poetry under the influence of surrealism. We are particularly interested in seeing such manuscripts from members of diverse and marginalized communities. Write Stuart at razovsky@ gmail.com.

*The Least You Can Do Is Be Magnificent: New & Selected Writings of Steve Venright,* compiled and with an afterword by Alessandro Porco (2017)
*I Heard Something,* by Jaime Forsythe (2018)
*On the Count of None,* by Allison Chisholm (2018)
*The Inflatable Life,* by Mark Laba (2019)
*Float and Scurry,* by Heather Birrell (2019)
*The Headless Man,* by Peter Dubé (2020)
*Queen and Carcass,* by Anna van Valkenburg (2020)
*il virus,* by Lillian Necakov (2021)
*Mouthfuls of Space,* by Tom Prime (2021)
*But the sun, and the ships and the fish, and the waves,* by Conyer Clayton (2022)
*Derelict Bicycles,* by Dale Tracy (2022)

**an imprint of Anvil Press**